E X P E C T A N C Y

It's never too late to change your game.

WILLIAM KEIPER

LIFE

EXPECTANCY

It's never too late to change your game.

Published by:
FirstGlobal Media dba FirstGlobal Partners LLC
7119 E. Shea Boulevard, Suite 109-177
Scottsdale, AZ 85254
LE@firstglobalpartners.com

Editing by: Chris Nelson, Kathryn Eimers Chandler and Steve Chandler
Cover design by: Brittany Alloway
Interior design by: Chris Nelson

FirstGlobal® website: www.firstglobalpartners.com

ISBN 978-0-9849893-0-0

Library of Congress Control Number 2011946120

First Edition, February 2012

For Pamala

'Come to the edge,' he said.
They said, 'We are afraid.'
'Come to the edge,' he said.
They came. He pushed them.
And they flew.

~ Guillaume Apollinaire

Contents

<u>With Appreciation</u>

- Steve Chandler: my coach and corner man, for creating with me and for his example of living boldly each and every day.

- Chris Nelson: for editing intelligence and creativity offered without arrogance.

- Kathryn Eimers Chandler: for copy editing precision, and for her kindness and faith.

- Brittany Alloway: for making design creativity look easy and getting it right the first time.

Your Train is Waiting...

Foreword

The great, poetic novelist John Updike talks about the "strange expectancy that getting on any train gives us." That's the same expectancy I felt when reading Will Keiper's first draft of this book.

Because prior to this book I'd known Will through his energetic, enthused conversations and, yes, I'll even say "rants" about what is happening in this world we are now living in. Will has clients all around the world, and as a well-known business consultant he is often asked to speak about trends and opportunities facing the world market today.

As he did his research for a speech one day, he came upon some alarming statistics. In short, he discovered, the world was not going to work. Not as planned. Not as we had complacently assumed, living off credit, inflated asset values, infinite benefits and governmental care and feeding. It no longer added up to a sustainable world. In fact, he found it an unsafe condition that would not mend itself.

But Will was not upset. In fact, he was excited. It was a whole new world and we all had a chance to get on board with the same strange (but invigorating) expectancy that we felt when boarding Updike's train.

As he talked to me about the speech he was preparing to give, I realized that my new duty to him as his friend was to urge him to write a book. I knew he had great ideas on many other topics, and I also knew his personal story was riveting. The way he'd turned his life around after a series of personal setbacks and financial challenges was remarkable.

It didn't take much persuading. This is a man who loves to write and who loves a challenge. And he had a clear vision. It was a vision for people of his generation—the baby boomers. He sees that many of them are in a very precarious situation at just the "wrong" time in their lives. He concludes that if they don't wake up to it, at some point in the not too distant future they'll be brutally blindsided by the reality of how insecure their future really is. But if they could wake up, there would be a great new adventure and a way to live out their retirement years in a much more active and fulfilling way.

What you will now be reading is the result of Will's profound whirlwind mind. It is the result of how he urgently jumps on a project and maximizes its potential rapidly. That's his business. Will is a turnaround artist in real life. He is hired by companies (and individuals) who are in distress and need help fast. Will enters and drives the making of bold, innovative, difficult decisions for them and then makes it happen with urgency. He is very successful at this kind of work and that experience has served him well in his approach to this book.

Because he's now applied himself and his special

brand of urgency to America, and, more specifically, the generation we call the boomers.

One of Will's professional roles when he enters stagnant organizations is that of truth-teller. People inside organizations often live within a complex, fearful web that makes telling the truth an uneasy and often unwelcome prospect. Will moves quickly. He knows that the truth is what will ultimately set them free. He delivers it with velocity and impact.

And he delivers the truth here, too, for those of us in the boomer generation who assumed we could be passive non-participants in life for our last twenty or so years. No longer true!

This book scared me, then woke me up, and then excited me about my future. Will does not spare us our mortality, our ignorance, our insolvency, our laziness, our immaturity or our lack of imagination. This truth hurts. But it is the very truth that can set our generation free.

But there is, throughout the book, a theme of positive expectancy. There are stories that inspire and reassure. There are solutions and ideas that rally the mind. Before I'd read this book I'd never thoroughly understood the concept of creative destruction. Now I do. What is happening is good and in some ways quite necessary. And now my future looks more adventurous than I ever thought possible.

Previously in America, "old people" surrendered their

liveliness and allowed the youth culture to dominate as they wasted away in retirement. Will Keiper has made the first strong argument for turning that paradigm on its head as the very solution to our country's problems. He declares a whole new game for us to play, and it's the opposite of fading away.

When Ralph Waldo Emerson wrote in his essay "Self-Reliance" that "Society is a conspiracy against the manhood of each of its members," it was a pronouncement that many felt was too extreme. But Will Keiper has given it new meaning, new urgency. Our old passive retirement society was a conspiracy against the manhood and womanhood of anyone over sixty-five. And "life expectancy" only meant a numerical calculation of years left before you pass away completely.

This book you are reading is a game-changer on that score. It reboots and refreshes the very word *expectancy*. Now it becomes, as one of my dictionaries proclaims, "That feeling of optimistic expectancy that fills theatergoers as they wait for the curtain to rise."

Steve Chandler
Phoenix, Arizona
February, 2012

Game-Changing for Mere Mortals

Introduction

The reasons for personal renewal and business transformation are as unique as the people and the companies seeking them. This book is about changing your life and work "games" for the better, no matter your current circumstances. It is about becoming the initiator of that change in the service of your best interests rather than continuing to be a reactor to the events around you. It is about being reflective and purposeful about your requirements and your direction.

My background includes CEO and board-level leadership for six U.S. public companies and a variety of others both domestic and global. My stock-in-trade is the ability to create highly beneficial shifts for businesses and individuals over very short periods of time. My ability to quickly see things differently and to tell the unvarnished truth about them—while rapidly moving into intensive action—has led me to work with people who have decided that the continuation of the status quo can't or won't be tolerated.

The American economic game and the associated stakes have substantially changed over the past couple of years. As a society, the financial, economic and social underpinnings of our country have undergone a sea change that will have a far-reaching and, I believe, decades-long impact.

In my view, *what was* in terms of the relative stability of the past thirty or forty years will not be seen again for a very long time. With seventy-five million children of the baby boom years moving through and past the age of sixty-five, the issues around aging and the period of life that used to be called the "retirement years" also have to be urgently and creatively addressed.

Many Americans will have more whitewater rapids than smooth sailing ahead for a long time to come. This kind of disruptive environment always holds significant opportunities to thrive or to merely survive. Those who can grasp the significance of the shift that has occurred—and who can take purposeful and timely actions in response to it—will get the best of the new options.

It is time to be a powerful agent of change in your own service or to engage another who can help guide you to a higher level of *game*. My objectives here are to suggest the power of mortality as a motivator, to offer my view of some of the dramatic changes in the American environment and address their implications, and to offer some ideas for how best to carve out your place going forward. Throughout *Life Expectancy*, I address principles that can drive purposeful change for individuals and businesses. My hope is to stimulate your thinking such that you will seize the opportunity to be a first-mover in this new era of uncertainty.

There is every reason to feel good about confronting and proactively restructuring your game no matter your age or the maturity of your business. Even if everything is going well for you at the moment, if you haven't changed your approach in a while that is a good reason to do it. It is never too late to be more proactive in the creation that is the rest of your life, and thereby get to the very top of your game.

William Keiper
Phoenix, Arizona
February, 2012

Chapter 1

28,452 Sunrises

Avoiding danger is no safer in the long run
than outright exposure. The fearful are caught
as often as the bold.
Helen Keller

First and foremost I am a pragmatist. Therefore the best of all places to begin the game-changing process is with a clear view of life expectancy.

If you could consciously comprehend the notion on the day of your birth, you would probably view the prospect of seeing 28,452 sunrises as a virtually limitless future. From that moment, though, the allotment of sand in the top of your brand new hourglass inexorably and silently drains away into the bottom of it.

Each day of your life thereafter the number of life-days behind you increases by one, while those ahead of you decrease by one. There is a seed of urgency and excitement and power in this understanding—an *expectancy*. As you will soon see, comprehension of life's end can be used to motivate actions that will increase the richness of your remaining years.

For a man celebrating his fortieth birthday today, his individual 'glass of life' has reached the point of being less than half full. For those of you who prefer looking through the other end of the telescope, his glass is now more than half empty. At forty, a man's average life expectancy consists of fewer days ahead than behind—the ones that cannot be recaptured.

The declining remainder of life is often pushed to your mind's forefront as a consequence of the loss of a loved one, your own brush with death, a debilitating illness or the specter of economic ruin. Absent these kinds of high-impact events, there may come a day when the reflection in your mirror simply looks back in a different, deeper way. You may recognize something that you hadn't seen or interpreted in the same way before. When will an awareness of the limited span of your own life move from somewhere deep in the recesses of your brain to the top of your mind, at least for a brief introduction?

Put another way, when will you consider the phrase *life expectancy*—the average time an individual is expected to live—in *personal* rather than *statistical* terms? Wouldn't you like to know approximately how many days you personally have remaining? Most of us either ignore this question or act as if the number is infinite. But no matter how you do it, acquainting yourself with the reality that your lifetime includes both a beginning and an end can be deeply empowering. It can motivate you to take important actions that may have long been procrastinated.

Seize Life

Steve Jobs, founder and longtime CEO of Apple, said, "Death is very likely the single best invention of life. It is life's change agent." The irony is that this realization is equally available and easily accessible to all of us. But we usually ignore the opportunity to use death as a motivator, as a means of creating a powerful sense of urgency that we can use to transform our lives. Why not raise the battle flag of *carpe vitam*—seize life—while you can? Use it in your own service and in your service of others. (See Chapter 18, *You're Gonna Have to Serve Somebody*. For more on Steve Jobs' remarkable story, see Chapter 5, *You Are Already Naked*.)

The Looking Glass

As a sixty-year-old male, the writing of *Life Expectancy* brought me face-to-face with my own mortality. My uncomfortable confrontation with and consequent acceptance of the outer limit of my remaining life will inevitably be repeated by tens of millions of aging American boomers at some point.

Acknowledgement of the absolute nature of my personal demise provided the inspiration to recommit to powerful change on a daily basis. This glimpse ahead also brought with it some discomfort and temporary sadness. Those feelings were largely non-specific but manifested as the aching of loss. Because of prior avoidance of the subject, I didn't have any context offering balance or perspective for what I was feeling. I got over the sadness though, and the commitment to really live remained.

* * *

It is ironic but somehow unsurprising that most of us spend more time thinking about and planning a vacation or a birthday party than we do about the aging process and its end point.

* * *

We don't typically consider the subject of mortality openly or even in private. Conventional wisdom and practice in the U.S. keeps death and its dimensions off-limits for day-to-day conversation. We don't talk about death except occasionally in the context of grief arising from the demise of an inner-circle relative, friend or acquaintance. When we hear about another's experience relating to the death of someone close, we say, "I am sorry for your loss," and then rapidly distance ourselves from the opportunity for a deeper conversation or exploration of the subject.

My acknowledgment of the existence of a final milepost ahead led me to learn more about the process of aging from a biological standpoint. Life expectancies for the boomer generation and those following it have increased, but the changes in our bodies as they are used for longer periods of time are quite predictable. Given the immediate access to information we all have at our fingertips, it won't take long for you to find for yourself the facts required to help you understand this routine but irreversible process—if you care to look.

When preparing for college or a move to a new city you look ahead, research the environment and try to close any gap between your expectations and the likely reality. Likewise, our knowledge gap can quickly be closed on the subject of the aging process and its logical conclusion. Why should it be any more of a mystery than any other process? Our individual DNA, character, experiences and physical manifestation are unique throughout our lives, but the final crossover instant from life to death is sameness personified.

Life's end is the symmetrical corollary of birth, but in our thoughts it typically remains abstract—remote and intangible. Birth is a festive welcoming; death represents for many a foreboding presence sometimes illustrated by the iconic Grim Reaper. For many, death remains the least likely event for celebration. We prefer to cling to the belief that our demise is not at all times *imminent*. We push away any intruding thoughts about the eventuality of the moment that is approaching with the consistent cadence of a funeral march. I did the same thing until now.

Memento Mori
(Remember, You Are Mortal)

Until now, I had almost without thinking considered my life on earth as a continuum with no end in sight. I now recognize that my belief was based upon willful ignorance rather than factual verification. It would have been a simple matter to look at any life expectancy chart and in about thirty seconds determine the years or even days likely remaining in my life.

Up to this point, my life had been spent simply addressing the challenges of each day. In particular I hadn't given much consideration to the stark reality of my earthly finish line. It took a series of unanticipated, adverse events to open my ears to the drumbeats counting down my remaining days—and to the fact that I alone have the power to actively and boldly determine how to spend them. I *awakened* at age sixty and *suddenly* discovered I had many fewer days ahead of me than I could have imagined. This fact had simply not been in my consciousness previously, nor was it a consideration in my decisions about how to spend each day or hour or even moment.

Each of us can do the simple arithmetic about life expectancy. In my case, I realized that at this point in my life there was every compelling reason not to hold back from actively making the most of the fleeting days, weeks and months I have remaining. I offer my learning and experience to you here as a potential shortcut to your own understanding. In particular I hope to lead you to the realization that changing your game *now* is important, timely (no matter your current age)—and entirely within your personal power. (For more on the power and importance of *now*, see Chapter 15, *Now is Your Present*.)

Time On Our Side

The oldest baby boomers—those born during the period 1946 to 1964—turned sixty-five during 2011. Because there are a lot more of us rapidly moving toward this milepost—I mean a *lot* of us—we will be hearing tens of millions of mortality alarms going off over the next several years. The triggers and the timing will be different, but the alarms will sound nonetheless.

Some of those born recently will enjoy New Year's Eve 2099 and the first day of the new century of 2100. However, as of 2050, of the more than *eighty-five million* Americans that will then be over the age of sixty-five, very likely *none of them* will go to that party. All of their lives will have ended prior to the year 2100.

(The associated probabilities suggest that a few of those who will have turned sixty-five by 2050 might make it to the dawning of 2100 at the very, very ripe old age of 114 or so. At this writing the oldest-known person in the world is believed to be Maria de Jesus of Portugal. She is 118.)

For most of us, blissful ignorance permits us to feel that "time is on our side." It is, of course—right up until the moment that it isn't. Time will go on undeterred, but eventually and without exception, each of us will be off-the-clock.

* * *

Why do most of us choose not to look closely at our

probable life expectancy? I suspect it is because we are not interested in the pain associated with discovering that we failed to fully use the precious days already written in our individual Books of Life.

* * *

And even if we want to recapture the past, we know in our hearts that we cannot ask for a "do-over" for any prior moment. The recognition of the facts about life expectancy may be sobering, but it is accompanied by the opportunity to take action and get the most out of the rest of life—starting now.

The starkness of the facts about mortality and how it is playing out across a generation of over seventy-five million Americans can be the best possible motivator to get you into action. If you want further motivation, by most counts more than ten percent of boomers of all ages passed away prior to age sixty-five.

While reading this chapter may be uncomfortable, it will be impossible to avoid repeatedly confronting the reality of the passing of your generational peers now and over the next several decades. You may want to rehearse your response to hearing word of the demise of someone you know, as you will repeatedly be called upon to offer condolences over the years ahead.

The surest way to shift your game of life *today* is to create it consciously and consistently with a purposeful vision of what you want it to be. You can unleash your talents, experience and wisdom to create and live the story of the unfolding of the rest of your life—*your* story. I call this active, creative process *changing your game.*

In order to provide yourself with even a bit more motivation to do this, I suggest you gently create space in your mind and heart for the consideration of your final milepost rather than leaving it for another day or year. I chose to look squarely at this reality. All of my days since then have been richer and more powerful, filled with more life than ever before. It can be the same for you.

Chapter 2

"Listen to Me, Dammit!"

The greatest hazard in life is to risk nothing.
The person who risks nothing, does nothing, has nothing,
and is nothing.
William Arthur Ward[1]

As humans we typically insist on experiencing things firsthand in order to imprint the deepest possible learning. Despite being told over and over, "Don't touch, it's hot!" a toddler will nonetheless reach up to make contact with a stovetop at least once. This real world experience assures it likely will never happen again.

As we get older we often *prefer* repeating the mistakes of those who came before us rather than trusting their advice. For ego protection, we would rather not appear inexperienced in the face of a problem; nor do we want to be perceived as unable or unwilling to directly confront it. Most of us would rather do anything *but* listen as the means to learn something. It makes no difference if our firsthand learning requires us to endure more pain or use more time and effort than might otherwise be necessary.

---

[1]The full text of the poem "Risks" by William Arthur Ward appears on page 243 of this book.

Would you consider an exception to this time-honored practice?

What if you had access to the consensus of a group of people over ninety-five years of age as to what they would most value if they had the opportunity to turn back the clock? I suggest that in the case of life wisdom offered by people who have survived well beyond the average life expectancy, hearing what they have to say (rather than making more unnecessary mistakes) would be preferable. Your future might benefit from listening to those who have already walked the path ahead of you. Hearing their words today might even preclude later regrets attached to not having a second chance at... (Complete the sentence with something you would prefer to not regret.)

In a talk entitled, "If I Had to Live it Over Again," Dr. Anthony Campolo, Professor Emeritus of Sociology at Eastern University (PA), references a sociological survey of fifty people, each of whom was at least ninety-five years old.[2] The single question asked was, "If you could live your life over, what would you do differently?" Some of the key findings were:

Take More Risks—They would have taken more risks when they had the opportunities to do so. The essence of the conclusion was that if they could re-set the clock to seventy-five or sixty (or even younger), they would now be prepared to move through their fear of taking more chanc-

---

[2]Tony Campolo. <http://tonycampolo.org/sermons/2000/01/if-i-had-to-live-it-over-again/>

es. They would welcome the opportunities they did not then seize to push themselves outside of their comfort zones... even if just a bit more.

If you are now fifty-five and you live to ninety-five, you have *forty years* of living ahead of you. At fifty-five, you are experienced, tested and probably wiser than in your youth. You likely no longer have minor children to raise. It is a choice available to you to make the years ahead the best and most productive of your life. What if you decided that just for the next month when your inner voice says, "No, I am not doing *that* because I haven't even started and it *already* feels uncomfortable," you instead say, "Just for this month I am going to try it, although it certainly feels uncomfortable." If a month is too long, try it for a week, or how about just a day?

How can you actively incorporate the advice of *take more risks* as you move through your life? Wouldn't it be great to be interviewed on *your* ninety-fifth birthday and be able to say, "I did everything I wanted to do by getting outside of my comfort zone—and I started doing it at age fifty-five!" The best could indeed be yet to come.

Be More Reflective—*They would have taken more time for reflecting about what was going on in their lives at the time, and how their decisions were either consistent or inconsistent with their values and priorities. They would have taken time to contemplate the deeper meaning of life, family, work, spirituality and much more, while in the process of living each day.*

If you are seventy-five and look ahead to being ninety-five, you have twenty years of opportunity to both do and reflect. Another option would be to watch a lot of TV, perhaps complain from time-to-time (or perpetually) about the seeming cruelty of the aging process and simply wait for the years to tick by. Then what? Regrets, rather than celebrating your mastery of those twenty years and the contributions you made and the wisdom you continued to cultivate?

It is all about perspective—being willing to believe that you are not winding down or checking out because you are fifty-five or seventy-five or eighty-two. You have a life ahead that can count for something if you choose to make a plan to change your game. It doesn't have to be deep or complicated. It just has to be your own creation supported by your commitment.

Create a Legacy—*They would have taken the opportunity to consider and create some kind of legacy, something that demonstrated that their lives counted in a way that would be remembered after they left this world.*

Your legacy could be the ongoing recognition of your positive influence and contributions by the people you have touched along the way. Your individual legacy could be the memory of your kindness to animals, or your charity and volunteer work. The thoughts of these fifty nonagenarians did not turn to wishing they had lost more weight, taken more vacations or even made more money. The answers were consistent no matter the respondent's prior occupation. By definition, it takes a while, but aging seems to represent a great social leveler.

The Downside of Risk

Risk is a word that carries with it an automatic but undeserved connotation of negativity.

* * *

But in truth it simply describes a situation that is not within the norm for you. The downside of risk is almost always overestimated. Unfortunately, confirmation of this almost always comes after the fact, when it is simply too late to act.

One man's risk is another's daily bread. Philippe Petit (celebrated in the film *Man on Wire*) walked, danced and even reclined on a cable he and his team surreptitiously strung between New York City's Twin Towers at 1,368 feet above the street. He did this for forty-five minutes and with a smile on his face. This would have been crazy for anyone else in the world, but he viewed it as an opportunity to showcase and celebrate his unique talent. For him it was a calculated risk with a lot of reputational upside for him as a professional wire-walker.

I see the nonagenarians' point about taking more risks as the most immediately relevant for boomers today. Pushing out of the comfort zone you may have occupied for years offers the best opportunity for enriching your life. In any event, given the economic developments of the past several years as well as the likely uncertain—if not rough—road ahead, your comfort zone is not the cozy place it once was and it may be worth escaping (or at least redecorating).

Most of us are going to have to create results that accommodate a significantly changed landscape. The old rules don't apply, and doing the things we have always done won't necessarily lead to the same once-predictable results.

Consider for a moment what you might be reflecting upon at age ninety-five: wouldn't it be a shame to look back and wish that you had taken slightly greater risks to have realized higher levels of satisfaction with your life—when you could still *do something* about it? The state of regret when you can do nothing to change your situation can be a terrible place in which to live.

What if you could make yourself really understand and appreciate this before making a decision to avoid a measured risk today? You can look back at your own life and find confirmation after confirmation that accepting a little more risk will often lead to unexpected gains. A review of your own experience will also confirm that taking little to no risk has a high probability of keeping you stuck.

If you are prepared to change your *game* (the creation of the rest of your life), make room for learning how to take risk-steps outside your comfort zone in a way that works for *you*. Give it some proactive thought when you have such a choice in front of you. Practice it. It doesn't mean you should walk on a high wire without a net (or at all) or that you shouldn't be smart and hedge your risks when and where you can.

Mark Twain said, "Twenty years from now you will be more disappointed by the things that you didn't do than by the ones you did." If you can internalize this wisdom now—without having to gain it through regret—your life will absolutely be richer. This conclusion is courtesy of people who lived to be over ninety-five years of age. When they had the opportunity to challenge themselves a bit more, they didn't do it. When they figured out that something was actually not as risky as they thought, it was simply too late to do anything about it.

A Legacy

A legacy that will be a lasting memory of your lifetime is worthy of reflection even as you deal with the more immediate, fundamental issues of life. Here are a few thoughts shared by Charles Murray in his lecture entitled "The Happiness of the People":

> To become a source of deep satisfaction, a human activity has to meet some stringent requirements. It has to have been important (we don't get deep satisfaction from trivial things). You have to have put a lot of effort into it (hence the cliché "nothing worth having comes easily"). And you have to have been responsible for the consequences.
>
> There aren't many activities in life that can satisfy those three requirements. Having been a good parent. That qualifies. A good marriage. That qualifies. Having been a good neighbor and good friend to those whose lives intersected with yours. That qualifies. And having been really good at

something—good at something that drew the most from your abilities. That qualifies.[3]

It is interesting that the points cited by Mr. Murray have to do with our humanity, our goodness and with simply finding and utilizing our special gifts. They are simple and personal and qualitative. They represent the elements of our uniqueness, not those of conformity. This understanding can be another major power source for changing your game. How can you leverage your uniqueness and ability and couple it with a powerful, ongoing personal commitment? How can you *now* move this consideration from an abstract concept into your reality of today?

The New Math: 90 = New 50, as 60 = New 30?

In an op-ed piece in *The New York Times*, Susan Jacoby referenced a panel discussion titled "90 Is the New 50," which was presented at the World Science Festival in 2008.[4] Researchers spoke to a middle-aged, standing-room-only audience about imminent medical miracles. Jacoby related that the one voice of caution about the inflated and misplaced expectations of 'turn-back-the-clock' aging was that of Robert Butler, a pioneering gerontologist who was the first head of the National Institute on Aging in the 1970s. He is generally credited with coining the term "ageism," which is

---

[3]Murray, Charles. 2009. *The Happiness of the People*. Aei Press.
[4]Jacoby, Susan. 2010. Real Life Among the Old. *The New York Times*, December 30, Opinion Pages.

defined as discrimination against middle-aged and elderly people.

A few months before Dr. Butler died from leukemia at age eighty-three, Ms. Jacoby asked him what he thought of the premise that ninety might become the new fifty. "I'm a scientist," he replied, "and a scientist always hopes for the big breakthrough. The trouble with expecting ninety to become the new fifty is it can stop rational discussion—on a societal as well as individual level—about how to make ninety a better ninety. This fantasy is a lot like waiting for Prince Charming, in that it doesn't distinguish between hope and reasonable expectation."

Ninety is not now and will never be the new fifty, just as sixty is not the new thirty. Making these kinds of claims is missing Dr. Butler's point that your life at your age today can be better than might have been the case had you been your current age twenty or thirty years ago. Our mission should be to create the best life we can at the ages we are today. The rest will take care of itself based upon what we do now, not what we would do if we were able to relive the days now passed.[5]

The responses of the nonagenarians about what *in hindsight* they view as important are as close to the truth of what matters most in life as you can get—without having

---

[5]By the way, if you aspire to live to 100, see: "11 Health Habits That Will Help You Live to 100" for more information. <http://health.usnews.com /health-news/family-health/living-well/articles/2009/02/20/10-health-habits-that-will-help-you-live-to-100>

celebrated at least your ninety-fifth birthday. These people had reached the point in their lives where there was absolutely no reason to sugarcoat anything. At their ages, the sand left in the top of their hourglasses didn't provide much opportunity for more start-ups, second chances or do-overs.

As you continue marching through your remaining life span, consider the conclusions of these near-centenarians when setting new goals and priorities for your life. Consider the things that you would do now if you were able to manage through a little discomfort and determine (or even just trust) that the associated risks very likely aren't as great as they may appear.

When you are ninety-five, would it make any difference to you if you could look back and see that you tried something and didn't succeed? What if you looked back and were able to see that you had tried, and then tried again, and actually succeeded? Taking action—a single step—is the key. *Trying* **is** actively doing. Who's to say that this mere action isn't success? At ninety-five (or even next week) wouldn't you prefer to look back at the actions you *took* rather than at your failures to even try?

Chapter 3

Baxie and the Vapor Trails

"Shane, why do you think animal lives are shorter than humans?" "People are born so that they can learn how to live a good life, like loving everybody all the time and being nice, right? Well, dogs already know how to do that, so they don't have to stay as long."
A six-year old on the passing of his dog, Belker

On a clear, 110° summer day in Arizona I went to a residence where the people were breeders of dogs known as Bichon Frises (pronounced "bee-shawn free-zays"). I was looking for a canine animal companion and had heard that this breed was friendly, mellow and bright.

The breeders had recently delivered several litters of these all-white, fluffy puppies. Almost thirty of them were running around outside. They were chasing and nipping at each other and rolling around like large-sized cotton balls with dark charcoal eyes. Despite the intense heat, they were vitally interested in playing the energetic games that came so naturally to them.

There was one puppy off by himself, lying in the shade with his body and his chin down in a little pool of water—which seemed really smart given the temperature. He looked comfortable enough, and clearly was not screaming by his actions, "Pick me, pick me!!" I liked the different drum that this little guy was hearing, so I picked him up and spent a few minutes with him. It was enough for me to know that he was for me. Little did I know until much later, that in a way that was his alone, *I* was actually selected by *him*. From that moment on, the newly-named *Baxter* and I were off and running on a joyful journey together.

Most dogs live life very much in the present, with the here and now in front of them at all times. Food, barking, other dogs and cats, water, naps, going outside (preferably), more food, more barking and naps, and so on. Baxter certainly enjoyed all of these aspects of his life.

In addition to being of the Bichon Frise persuasion, Baxter was also a masterful chowhound who perpetually assumed the role of chief taster for everyone in the house. He was a canine "foodie" and was completely open to the entire universe of savory scents and tastings. He also saw it as his sworn duty to protect the dog food bowl from all others, including the other three canine companions in the house. He spent hours resting in front of it—with one eye at least partially open—making sure neither it nor its contents disappeared without his express permission.

Sky Pilot

Baxter though, had a bigger vision than that which was right in front of him. He was gifted in a very unique way.

High flying military jet airplanes cannot always by seen by the naked eye, but they can often be detected by the vapor trails visible behind the unseen aircraft. Baxter had the ability to find these trails from the ground, regardless of whether the visible part of a trail was long, short, or a mere dot in the sky. He would sound the alarm for all of us by throwing his head back and giving a throaty bark, as if pointing at the trail and saying, "Hey, you've got to check this out." He did this from the time he was about a year old.

He and I walked ten or fifteen miles a week together for years. We were well known in our neighborhood as the tall guy and the "...adorable white dog that always looks as though he is smiling." Everyone knew Baxter by name—a recognition that wasn't afforded to me. As he got older he was still always ready to walk, but was slowing down a bit— some days a lot more stopping, sniffing and peeing than actual walking.

He suddenly became ill and went into a rapid decline. After several days in the care of our vets, a sonogram revealed he had managed to swallow—but had not digested—a cloth object of some sort that was blocking everything. Though it meant surgery at a time when he was not at his best, I was relieved that it seemed to be nothing more serious. He had immediate surgery to remove the blockage (a Victoria's Secret thong stealthily taken from the laundry room with the intention of it being buried in the back yard), and in a couple of days was released back to our care.

He seemed to be recovering nicely for a little while, at

least by comparison to what life was like for him immediately before the surgery. Before long though, it became clear that something else was wrong. After an exhaustive diagnostic effort, our vets discovered that Baxter had a rare kind of slow-growing cancer that only rears its ugly head when it is too late to do anything about it. I asked, "How long does he have?" and the vet answered, "It's very hard to say, but probably less than a week."

The news was devastating. I scooped him up and took him home, determined to give him the most comforting and loving five or six days of his life. But it was not to be. After a completely sleepless and very difficult first night back at home, it became clear that my Baxter was out of days. It was over for him and it was over for us. The end of our deeply bonded human-animal companion connection had suddenly arrived. I softly whispered, "Good-bye sweet boy," and through the rain of my tears I could see that his unique and beautiful spark was gone.

My Teacher

It made no difference that he was an animal companion rather than a human companion—his death was a poignant reminder of the fragility of life and the immediate void created by the separation at death.

As it turned out, Baxter's passing taught me much about loss and grief for a loved one. He provided me with the unexpected gift of an opportunity to both experience and relate to his mortality. Right or wrong, I viewed his death as a proxy for my own and a reminder that life's end isn't at all predictable.

In my purposeful ignorance, I actually thought Baxter might live to celebrate his twenty-fifth birthday. I envisioned him being thrilled on that day as he observed a flyover by the Air Force Blue Angels (arranged by me, of course) filling the sky with a fireworks-like display of incredible vapor trails.

None of us has the ability to avoid seeing the end points of lives all around us. We cannot know whether we will stick around to see the far side of the life expectancy curve or whether we will be among those whose premature deaths bring down the average. This is all the more reason to follow the advice of the nonagenarians to *take more risks* and find even small ways to do so every day. Since no loved one can be brought back—no matter the *genus*—we have compelling reasons to be bold each and every day while we are here.

I was fortunate to experience life with Baxter for fourteen years (for him, the rough equivalent of eighty-five human years). He had unexpectedly unique vision and celebrated it almost every clear and sunny day. He could see what others couldn't. His world was different from, and certainly much bigger than, most of the other canines (and many of the humans) I have known. He discovered his unique gift and never noticed nor cared that other dogs didn't see what he could see.

* * *

We all have undiscovered gifts that can help us create and address new opportunities and horizons. How can you utilize, leverage and celebrate your unique talents as a part of changing your game? What is the point of leaving any energetic fuel in your tank?

* * *

As Baxter so often conveyed to me in his deep canine voice, "So many vapor trails—so little time." No waiting. No stopping. Simple. Living.

Chapter 4

Your Twenty-Five-Year Life

It is not the strongest of the species that survive,
nor the most intelligent,
but rather the one most adaptable to change.
Clarence Darrow

If you were born today and could comprehend that your full life span was going to be just twenty-five years, how would you choose to spend it?

If today was in fact your *birth* day, you would by definition have neither the experience nor the developed thinking processes required to make responsible choices. As a newborn with a mere twenty-five-year life span ahead, your life's end would very likely be full of regret simply because of your inability to comprehend the choices available to you soon enough to make much of a difference.

If you are forty-five or even sixty today, your remaining lifetime could realistically be twenty-five years. It could be more of course, or even less. As an adult versus a newborn you have both decision-making capacity and life experience to support your choices. Also, I suspect that with forty-five or sixty years of living behind you, it is unlikely you would now view a twenty-five-year period as a *limitless future* and might therefore be more judicious in how you spend your time.

As we get older, blocks of time can be measured by events in our own history that seem as though they took place "just yesterday." We sometimes further contextualize these by recalling who the president was or whether some major world events or calamities were happening at the time. Years (even mere *summers*) that seemed interminably long in youth absolutely race by as we get older. "Is it New Year's Eve again—already?"

* * *

You can infuse your choices with greater meaning by placing them in the context of having fewer than twenty-five years within which to both decide and to act on the things of importance to you.

* * *

You have the opportunity to spend the rest of your life *however you choose,* whether your life's end is at seventy or eighty-five; simply add twenty-five years to your current age to put this concept into high relief.

If you knew today that your life was going to time out twenty-five years from now, would you change your game of life in any way? If so, how would you change your approach to get results different from those you have been getting? Could you utilize the concept of *minimizing future regrets* as a way of motivating yourself to drive your own game up a notch or two? The desire to avoid future regrets can be a powerful motivator for moving into action *now*. If you are really adventuresome, project *a fifteen- or ten-year life*. Would you stick with your current course without changing, or at least challenging, any part of it?

"Regrets? I've Had a Few...But Then Again, Too Few to Mention"[6]

Is there anything worse than finding that when you recall certain people and events in your life, the thoughts that come to mind about them are tinged with regret? "I wish I had..." or "If only..." or "My life would be so different today if..." Can you recall an approach to another person that you should have made? Anger or unkindness toward another being, human or otherwise? Things left unsaid to a person no longer here? Leaving when you might have stayed? Friend-ships left untended or abandoned? The memory may arise accompanied by a wince or a sigh, perhaps even a tear. In any event, there always seems to be a kind of *emptiness* associated with the feeling of regret.

It will probably not surprise you that recent research suggests the most common regret among American adults involves a lost romantic opportunity. Columnist Tara Parker-Pope of *The New York Times* wrote about a report by re-searchers at Northwestern University and the University of Illinois at Urbana-Champaign who collected data from 370

---

[6]Anka, Paul (lyrics); François, Claude and Revaux, Jacques (composers). 1969. "My Way"; Burbank, CA: Reprise Records.

adults in the United States during a telephone survey. She wrote:

> They asked respondents to describe one memorable regret, explaining what it was, how it happened and whether their regret stemmed from something they did or didn't do.
>
> The most common regret involved romance, with nearly one in five respondents telling a story of a missed love connection. The second most common regret involved family issues, with 16 percent of respondents expressing regret about a family squabble or having been unkind to a sibling as a child.[7]

If you consider the ninety-five year olds and their expressed regrets, they collectively offered powerful perspectives on what could have been done differently in their lives when they had the chance. With the passage of time, these feelings of *what might have been* may become aches that are simply impossible to eliminate. It would be such a shame in our older years to feel such regrets as haunting echoes of the past.

Can there be any endeavor more worthwhile for a person of any age than to ask these kinds of questions: "How will I feel in the twilight of my life if I don't do or see or say or pursue this today?" "How might I feel if I don't stop this or gain control of that?" "What would it be like in my later years to know that I am powerless to address something I view as important to me?" "Will there be a greater feeling of regret

---

[7]Parker-Pope, Tara. 2011. What's Your Biggest Regret? *The New York Times*, March 23, Health section.

attached to what I *did* or *did not* do?"

If asking and answering these kinds of questions will allow you to take action in your best interest—and to do so now—use them. In fact, use whatever tools, tricks, cleverness, affirmations or other motivators you need to in order to take the step that is so vital to a life worth celebrating. The possibility-step that takes you to a new perspective: the *first* step.

A Regret Sampler

As you develop your approach to actively change the game you have been playing up until now, take a little time to put into perspective the living you have already done. If there are things about which you have feelings of regret today, or which you can imagine feeling regret about when you are older, acknowledge them now. You can then choose to do something to address them immediately (if the possibility remains), or you can make a commitment to *release those feelings now* in order to give more power to your present.

In this book I offer my thoughts and insights about actions that could be taken now and in your future to serve you in changing your game no matter your age. The corollary is that these actions, if not taken, could end up in your *well of regret* at some point down the line.

Most of us need little or no help when it comes to formulating statements of regret, but I offer a few that relate to the themes of this book:

- "I counted on retirement as an entitlement. I didn't prepare to continue living and working in the main-stream—I haven't kept up-to-date on the technology that everyone is using."

- "I trusted in others to protect my assets and my income potential, and I failed to take control of my own financial well-being. I didn't realize that the dollar had fallen so much that the real value of my savings was actually declining."

- "Although I was generally aware of the aggregate political power of the boomer generation, I stayed on the sidelines and didn't add my efforts or my voice to influence the key issues impacting my life. I didn't think I even needed to vote."

- "I ignored the opportunity to move toward greater self-reliance in the misplaced belief that someone or something would look after me. I paid into Social Security for more than forty years—I thought that was a savings account I could count on. Now I'm not sure."

- "I avoided looking at the reality of my mortality, and didn't use it as a motivator for intentional living when I had the opportunity. If I had had a higher degree of awareness about it when I was forty-five, my life today would be so much better."

- "I didn't consider until it was too late that I might care about being remembered for *something* about my life on earth. I could have contributed my efforts to something important instead of wasting tens of thousands of hours on _____."

- "I didn't value the significant people in my life, including my immediate family, the way I should have, and in the way they deserved. I am growing old in peace and quiet but I now want more people (and less of the silence) in my life."

- "I avoided exploring and finding my personal uniqueness and harnessing it in the service of others. I can now see how offering to be of service could have led to many opportunities. Now there is no point in even trying—it's too late for me."

- "I deferred making decisions until it was too late, or I made decisions through my inaction. In truth, I was a procrastinator. Now I am not sure I know how to do anything other than doing what I've always done: wait for things to happen to me."

- "I failed to create even a bare outline for the creation of the rest of my life until many years and opportunities had passed me by. Now I don't know how to start, or even if it is worth the bother. I don't have the energy I once did."

You can certainly add to these, or turn them into paragraphs or pages. You shouldn't expect for all or even most of them to apply to you. The question is: Is there something you can and want to do about those which you could envision someday applying to you? If not, you can close the book on that situation or relationship or consequence. If, however, there is a seed of regret or a real possibility of it in the future, make a place for dealing with it in the creation of your plan for changing your game. Take the opportunity to avoid some of those inconsolable feelings that might one day leave you pining for the past—wishing and hoping for that which can no longer be recovered.

Although I have said regret can be a motivator for some people, in my personal view it is a waste of valuable time and energy that can be better used. I see regret as a form of self-inflicted pain that once recognized needs to be released as soon as possible. Hanging on to it gets in the way of being better able to focus on today and develop readiness for tomorrow. Unlike chronic physical pain, the pain of regret is within your control to relinquish: "Regret! I have done all I can with you; good riddance."

Or you could choose to diminish regret into nothingness by reducing it to the extreme of absurdity offered by Woody Allen: "My one regret in life is that I am not someone else." Once you have embraced that *regret of all regrets*, you can really get on with your life—even if you have to pretend to be someone else!

Move Yourself in *Any* Direction

What best moves you from inactivity into action? How can you learn to seize your available opportunities *today*? You must act on the premise that approaching things differently from how you have in the past will yield different results in the future. Different and very likely *better*, based upon your deeper experience, wisdom, capacity for reflective thinking and purposeful decision making. All of these attributes exist at least in part based upon the passage of time. Moving into a different and higher gear—or at least out of neutral—is the starting point. *You* know best how to do this for yourself.

If the avoidance of potential regret can work for you as a motivational tool—use it. If fear of failure, or not having enough, or losing this, or escaping that—works for you in the creation of your future—use it. If positive affirmations work for you—use them. If a system of rewards works for you—use it. ("When I lose five pounds, I am going to Dairy Queen." While enjoying your treat, set another goal.) Moving yourself into a position to really *change your game* is the objective.

Set yourself up for success by plugging into your most powerful personal motivators for action. You already know what they are. Among them could be an incentive or a psychological tool you discovered long ago that *simply works* for you. Use it to take that very first step toward action.

It Can't Be Helped

"Everything happens for a reason" is a timeworn phrase for abdicating responsibility for anything that you have not done well, or have left undone, in your life. This phrase is almost never applied to something that has resulted in a positive outcome. When said among a group there is often an empathetic wave of head wagging because everyone wants to believe that this pabulum is true. In my view, use of this phrase is a fatalistic cop-out. It moves your mind and heart into neutral—to a place permitting absolution without thinking for all actions taken and all choices not made. It turns what could be a vibrant life into a sort of inanimate object to be observed, rather than something in which you are the prime actor and over which you have a good deal of power.

Things don't "just happen," at least not most of the time. Choices drive consequences. Plan to make the best choices you can *in the present*. If you later feel they were "wrong", fix the ones you can, and do so as soon as you become aware of the need to do so.

Opportunity Everywhere

The state of permanent disruption in which we must live the rest of our lives is actually very exciting. There is opportunity everywhere you look because of the change in our economic and social dynamics.

Just because these changes are viewed by some as

"bad" or "negative" doesn't mean that you have to go along with this perspective of the world. As a sort of *positive contrarian* you can discover *your way* of getting the results that will serve your best interests in your current circumstances.

While others are paying tribute to statements like: "I am sure things will get back to normal pretty soon" or "The worst is over" or "When the new president is elected things will really change" or "I think I'll just wait a while before I take any action—the passage of time heals everything," you can actually *be in action*, spending your time creating what you choose for the rest of your life.

And there is no "societal norm" for living one's life. Even if there was, isn't it time to create the rest of your life as you see fit without reference to what hordes of conformists may be doing? Consider yourself in possession of a blank slate to write on. Nothing that has come before need be accepted as a reason why "you can't do that."

Viktor Frankl, author of *Man's Search for Meaning*,[8] writes, "Live as if you were living a second time, and as though you had acted wrongly the first time." When you place this attitude into the context of having a mere twenty-five year lifetime for planning *and* playing out the rest of your days, you may well discover the personal power and commitment to urgency to make it happen in the way that you choose.

---

[8]Frankl, Viktor, *Man's Search for Meaning*. 2006. Boston: Beacon Press.

Chapter 5

You Are Already Naked

*Here is the test to find whether your mission
on Earth is finished: if you're alive, it isn't.*
Richard Bach

During the early days of my career in business, I found myself near the vortex of the development and growth of the personal computer industry.

I was fortunate to be president of a company in the business of distributing early-generation personal computers and related products, such as printers, monitors, software and networking products. The company grew very rapidly over a period of five years (from a small company to over $1.5 billion in annual revenue) and required me to develop new skills, including rapid planning and the creation and implementation of new programs and processes on a continuous basis. This gave me my start in thinking about and testing the creativity, strategic thinking and game-changing concepts addressed in *Life Expectancy*.

Finding myself in the middle of this brave new digital world filled with a continuous stream of innovative products and technology, I became acquainted with many interesting and unique people. Included among these were some who later became part of the royalty of the personal computer industry: Bill Gates of Microsoft, Don Estridge of the IBM PC organization, Ray Noorda of Novell, and Steve Jobs of Apple. If there were a Mt. Rushmore of the PC industry, it would not be difficult to visualize the faces of these four individuals carved in granite.

The Stanford Sermon for the Ages

Steve Jobs had supernatural success with Apple, NeXT, Pixar and a variety of other companies. He was one of the highest profile stories of amazing creativity, spectacular success and awe-inspiring resilience. But one of his best pieces of work was the hard-earned wisdom he shared in a commencement speech to the 2005 graduates of Stanford University.

In the process of planning and creating the next chapter in changing my own game, I revisited this inspirational speech. In it, Jobs detailed many important lessons garnered from his experience, revealing a side of him many had not seen before. In offering an unsentimental view of his life and career, he illuminated some of the important challenges, setbacks, and achievements that made him the person he was at that moment. More importantly, he shared the lessons he learned along the way. His advice about some of the truly important things in life is relevant for all thinking people.[9]

---

[9]You can see and hear the entire speech at http://www.youtube.com/watch?v=UF8uR6Z6KLc. The full text can be read at: www.stanford.edu/

I wish I could claim some of his words as my own, but since I cannot, I offer a few excerpts that I am certain will be relevant should you choose to change your game of life.

Jobs said, "Remembering that I'll be dead soon is the most important tool I've ever encountered to help me make the big choices in life. Because almost everything—all external expectations, all pride, all fear of embarrassment or failure—these things just fall away in the face of death, leaving only what is truly important. Remembering that you are going to die is the best way I know to avoid the trap of thinking you have something to lose. You are already naked. There is no reason not to follow your heart."

He also said, "for the past 33 years, I have looked in the mirror every morning and asked myself: 'If today were the last day of my life, would I want to do what I am about to do today?' And whenever the answer has been 'No' for too many days in a row, I know I need to change something."

He continued, "No one wants to die. Even people who want to go to heaven don't want to die to get there. And yet death is the destination we all share. No one has ever escaped it. And that is as it should be, because Death is very likely the single best invention of Life. It is Life's change agent. It clears out the old to make way for the new. Right now the new is you, but someday not too long from now, you will gradually become the old and be cleared away. Sorry to be so dramatic, but it is quite true."

He concluded with the following: "Your time is limited, so don't waste it living someone else's life. Don't be trapped by dogma—which is living with the results of other people's thinking. Don't let the noise of others' opinions drown out your own inner voice. And most important, have the courage to follow your heart and intuition. They somehow already know what you truly want to become. Everything else is secondary."

The Next Chapter

When he offered those remarks he had been battling pancreatic cancer for a year, including the completion of a significant surgical procedure. He had a liver transplant after this (in 2009), and contended with other illnesses that kept him on the Apple sidelines for several extended periods. There was never any question that as strong as his commitment was to his work and creative endeavors, he would only continue contributing if he felt he could give it his all—his very best.

On August 24, 2011, the moment arrived when he could no longer continue leading Apple with the energy he had devoted to it for so long. He submitted a letter of resignation to the Apple board of directors in which he said, "I have always said if there ever came a day when I could no longer meet my duties and expectations as Apple's CEO, I would be the first to let you know. Unfortunately, that day has come."[10]

Born in 1955—right in the middle of the baby boom—his torch had burned brightly for decades. He likely accomplished more—and had a greater impact on personal digital technology—than any other boomer. If he had more to give, I am sure that he would have done everything in his power to do so. There are many, many examples of highly visible celebrities, entertainers and athletes who stayed too long, or came back too frequently, despite being unable to deliver the goods that made them truly great at one time. I respect the fact that Steve Jobs walked away when he could still do so with his head held high, his dignity 100% intact.

Jobs' sharing of his life lessons was beautiful and compelling in its honesty and openness. Listen to your inner voice as you consider your choices for spending the remainder of your very valuable and limited life. Think about how you would fill in the blank: *Life is too short not to* _____. And then set about doing it. Steve Jobs' life was a powerful example of high-level performance despite huge challenges. His personal objectivity and discipline were at their best in making the decision to step aside at the appropriate moment.

An Amazing Torch

On October 5, 2011, Steve Jobs lost his fight with the

---

[10]See the full text of the letter: http://bits.blogs.nytimes.com/2011/08/24/text-of-jobss-resignation-letter/

wasting illness that had dogged him since 2004. Dr. Dean Ornish, one of Jobs' longtime physicians, was quoted in *The New York Times* following Jobs' death, "for Steve, it was all about living life on his own terms and not wasting a moment with things he didn't think were important. He was aware that his time on earth was limited. He wanted control of what he did with the choices that were left."[11]

Steve Jobs through personal experience came to possess a profound understanding of the value of irretrievable time. We should all aspire to reach this same kind of awareness, an understanding that we have the same power, the same opportunity to make choices and do so in a timely manner.

After Jobs' death, my thoughts turned to him as a teenager in the 1960s and early 1970s, and of the rock concerts of that era, some of which he undoubtedly attended. The celebration of his life reminded me of the tradition of concertgoers celebrating the end of a great concert by holding lighters aflame high above their heads. When this happens, the individual flames appear like so many stars in a night sky. They offer communal, silent recognition of what has just been witnessed.

Today I imagine tens of millions of Apple iPhones, iPods and iPads held aloft, their screens aglow with the images of burning candles. Such a tribute befits this digital rock star and pioneer of personal computing technology.

---

[11]Duhigg, Charles. 2011. With Time Running Short, Jobs Managed His Farewells. *The New York Times*, October 6, Technology section.

George Bernard Shaw could well have had Steve Jobs in mind when he wrote *A Splendid Torch*. Here is an excerpt from Shaw's powerful work:

> This is the true joy in life, the being used for a purpose recognized by yourself as a mighty one; the being a force of nature instead of a feverish, selfish little clod of ailments and grievances complaining that the world will not devote itself to making you happy . . . I want to be thoroughly used up when I die, for the harder I work the more I live. I rejoice in life for its own sake. Life is no "brief candle" for me. It is a sort of splendid torch which I have got hold of for the moment, and I want to make it burn as brightly as possible before handing it on to future generations.

When Steve Jobs' torch was extinguished he had irrevocably changed the world of personal digital technology for hundreds of millions of people around the globe. By following his heart he assured that his influence will be felt for generations to come.

Chapter 6

The Lifetime Warranty

I pay no attention whatever to anybody's praise or blame.
I simply follow my own feelings.
Wolfgang Amadeus Mozart

Keeping a productive place in society can take many forms. At ninety-one, Marius Carter (Blackie) Plummer went shopping for a new John Deere tractor he could use to get around his farm in Texas.

He found the one he wanted and was told that it came with a two-year standard warranty. He asked the salesman, "How much for the lifetime warranty?" His seventy-two-year-old son intervened and said, "Dad, don't you think the standard warranty will be sufficient at your age?" Blackie retorted, "I'll pay extra for the extended warranty—you just never know. I don't want to have to come up with more money for service after the two years are up..."

Blackie neither knew nor cared that the actuarial tables read that a man of ninety-one has a miniscule portion of life remaining. He saw no point whatsoever in allowing his attitude about living to be influenced by when the warranty on his vehicle would expire. It didn't even register in his consciousness that he would not productively ride that tractor for years to come. His plan was to live to ride that tractor with no end in sight. That was his place and his choice and his life, and it engendered the feeling that he wanted to have every day of his life

Between the time he took delivery of the new tractor and the day he died, he climbed up on that shiny green John Deere and drove it every single day. As far as he was concerned, he was living large riding that tractor around his property. He also loved that he never had to pay an extra penny for parts and labor. When he died just after his *ninety-eighth* birthday, he passed his prized possession on to his son, Marius Carter (Mack) Plummer.

"When I Get Old..."

Mack has had cancer, his gall bladder was removed and he is nearly blind in one eye. He battles diabetes every day. He still has a vivid picture of his dad sitting up on that tractor, spry, happy, fully engaged in life and feeling good about himself—through his late nineties.

Though not quite as robust as his dad, on his next birthday Mack will be eighty-two. He sits in his recliner with his dog Saylor stuck to him like Velcro and still buys, fixes up and sells dozens of houses every year. And, he doesn't worry about when the houses will sell. In terms of attitude, he recently found a small house that he liked very much, and said, "I want to have this one *for when I get old...*"

He has found a way of living and staying engaged in

the world that works for him. He is authentic, honest and unique. It doesn't matter to him where he lives or what he wears or how much money he has. He daily creates a life that for him is precisely what he wants it to be. At eighty-one, he still makes a living working from his easy chair with Saylor as his canine "assistant." It feels good to him, and that is what matters. He doesn't have the need to prove anything to anyone else. He owns his self-reliant life.

How Does It Feel?

You don't have to wait until you're eighty or ninety to fiercely *own* your life.

Sometimes you can more immediately access this ownership when you find it in the *feeling* rather than the *thinking* part of you. For example, when we are deciding whom we want to spend time with, we often try to make our decision rationally, based on factors like a person's perceived social or business standing, or on an idea of what they can "do for us." Rarely do we ask ourselves how we will likely *feel* when we are spending the time we have committed.

In fact, our decisions about how to spend our precious time are often made without much self-examination at all. How many times after coming home from an event—a dinner party, for example—do you say to your partner, "We should have stayed home. I felt so uncomfortable being with them tonight—remind me to just say 'no thanks' next time"? Could you have saved yourself the grief—and made a decision not to go—by checking in with your feelings ahead of time?

My daughter MacKenzie has an approach to this issue that belies her fifteen years. She continuously processes how, where and with whom she spends her time by using the "how does it feel" test. She calibrates her internal feel-good-meter and applies it to each situation she confronts. If it doesn't pass the threshold on her scale, she opts out of going, or of staying longer if she is already there.

She does this without judgment about anyone else and without regard for what she might be missing. She also acts on her own in the face of peer pressure—a big deal when you are a teenager. Her process involves simply examining and trusting her feelings. If she happens to get into a situation that doesn't feel good, she lets us know and we immediately pick her up wherever she is—no questions asked (well, maybe just a few). When we get home she usually retreats to the sanctuary of her bedroom, where she is quite content to spend time with her own thoughts (and of course Facebook).

You might refer to this process as checking your "crap detector." As adults, we find ourselves spending time in the pursuit of people and events and things that later seem pointless, or worse. There is something beautifully honest about just examining the feeling that is there, and if you do so in advance you can often spare yourself unnecessary regrets. You can assess ahead of time whether there is any value in spending even a small portion of your remaining life in situations that simply don't fit into your feelings of value or goodness. You *do* have a choice as to how to spend every hour of your remaining life.

I am proud of MacKenzie for making such a strong personal commitment. I am also impressed that she doesn't put herself in the all too familiar adult position of second-guessing her choices after the fact. (I wish my own DNA was stronger in this category.) She is defining her own life moment-by-moment, informed by an awareness of the passage of time, and not based on anybody else's expectations. Self-reliance is in her genes, and it manifests itself through her choices even as a teen. (By the way, her great-grandfather was Blackie Plummer. Mack is her granddad.)

* * *

When things have gone well for you in the past, when you seemed to be in a "zone" of positivity, producing results and staying out of your own way, how did it feel? What were you tapping into that enabled you to be engaged in ways that you ordinarily are not?

* * *

If you are going to change your game, you must first make the commitment to do it and then recommit to it every day. Own it. Otherwise you'll simply be a part of other people's games. And haven't most of us already danced to others' tunes for too long?

Chapter 7

Feel Free to Remove Your Mask

Man is least himself when he talks in his own person.
Give him a mask, and he will tell you the truth.
Oscar Wilde

We love self-disclosure when other people are engaging in it.

It provides the best vicarious, risk-free (and often self-indulgent) opportunity to judge another person's life situation against your own subjective scorecard. Depending on the depth of disclosure, it can range from interesting to entertaining to the equivalent of watching the aftermath of a train wreck. *It may be tragic, but you can't help slowing down to get a better look as you pass by.*

If you have honestly engaged in this kind of disclosure, you know it's harder than it looks. But to those listening, your own life-learning represents the most unique and interesting part of you. Nobody else can offer what you can: your individual history, the sum total of your cumulative life experiences. Your history is as unique as your fingerprints. Other people can learn from it, from the choices made or not made, from how our decisions worked or didn't, and maybe they will even hear something in our openness that will be of value to them in their life today or in the future.

The True Truth

By most standards I have had many successes in terms of career, education, athletics, parenting and in reaching a level of mastery in certain of my interests. Often I was the leader of this, the conceiver of that, and the force initiating and pushing along the other thing. I served as president, CEO or chairman of a number of U.S. public companies. I have traveled to many of the major capitals of the world. I made well over a million dollars during a number of years of my working life.

But when I searched for my real truth (I guess that is as opposed to the "false truth", which is rather ironic) I discovered it to be somewhat different than I expected.

I found my personal history littered with high-sounding, *almost* bulletproof rationalizations for why my obsessive pursuit of change of almost any kind during my adult life was such a great idea at the time. These changes involved relationships, employment, homes, cities and states and a lot of other things. In so doing, I expended tremendous time, money and valuable energy. Even my rationalizations consumed a lot of energy. As Mark Twain said, "It's no wonder that truth is stranger than fiction. Fiction has to make sense."

Looking back, it is clear to me that some of the energy expended could have been harnessed in the purposeful, and maybe even optimal, use of my ever-diminishing life-days (and certainly could have supplied the power for a small city for at least a few weeks). My truth may not in fact be as extreme as it now sounds even to me. But I can still make the case that the approach I took was dysfunctional enough to want it left behind me for good.

On the other hand, my experiences led me to the formulation of the principles and approaches set forth in these pages. For me, confronting and dealing with change became second nature—something to be embraced, not feared or avoided. My experiences gave me the tools to master the process of leading people and businesses through necessary change—and the ability to address problems and get moving in the direction of solutions almost immediately.

As I am now painfully aware, spent energy can never be recaptured. When I began thinking in terms of how I would choose to value my remaining life, I committed to myself that I would maintain a high level of awareness of the cost of misdirected energy and ill-considered priorities. My intention now is to be one of those boomers at the front of the pack, and as a consequence, capture a few of the best available opportunities that fit well with my positive attributes and uniqueness.

I am now in the habit of proactively thinking and planning what I will do and create *today*. I also know it is possible for me to make a difference for others *and* serve my economic interests at the same time. In fact, it doesn't usually work out very well if this mutuality of exchange is not present. (See Chapter 18, *You're Gonna Have to Serve Somebody.*) This approach also allows me to challenge the currents of conventional wisdom and public opinion and make my own independent choices (even if my logic may at times escape everyone else).

* * *

The finding of your own truth for illuminating the path ahead isn't for or about anyone else. It is simply a process of you doing your best to determine what is true for you, examining what you find, and acting on the conclusions that are of highest value.

* * *

Why are you who and where you are today, and where might you be able to go with the understanding of this truth about yourself? Ask yourself if what you have perceived as your truth is really true. What if it is (or isn't)? It takes an understanding of what has obstructed you in the past (including your own actions) to be able to create from a present unburdened by that history. In order to create results different from those still visible in your rearview mirror, a kind of ruthless self-examination is mandatory.

As we move toward a focus on changing your game from the inside out—from here to the end of this book— please begin considering the question, "What is my truth, and which parts of it may need revision?" And as suggested by Oscar Wilde in the quote at the beginning of this chapter, you might find it useful to wear a mask to get to it.

"Learning" Not "Failure"

The words success and failure are loaded terms, oozing subjectivity and judgment. This is true even when echoing in our own minds, especially those who make it their business to be both their best and worst critics. Any outcome can be viewed as both a success and a failure depending on the individual or group doing the scoring, and their familiarity (or lack thereof) with all of the circumstances contributing to the result. Given this high degree of subjectivity (and even so-called quantitative measures are often based upon subjective assumptions) and the fact that success and failure are separated by only a few degrees, why do we typically celebrate successes and diminish our failures?

Some of the best learning we have available is readily accessible in a review of experiences we may long have counted as "failures" and might rather forget. Tina Seelig, a Stanford University professor, conducts a class in creative thinking and is the author of *What I Wish I Knew When I Was Twenty: A Crash Course on Making Your Place in the World*.[12] As part of one of her courses she requires her students to write a resume of their perceived failures. She says,

A failure resume is a quick way to demonstrate that failure

---

[12]Seelig, Tina. *What I Wish I Knew When I Was 20: A Crash Course on Making Your Place in the World*. 2009. New York: HarperOne.

is an important part of our learning process, especially when you're stretching your abilities, doing things the first time, or taking risks. We hire people who have experience not just because of their successes but also because of their failures. Failures increase the chance that you won't make the same mistake again. Failures are also a sign that you have taken on challenges that expand your skills. In fact, many successful people believe that if you aren't failing sometimes then you aren't taking enough risks. Additionally, it is pretty clear that the ratio of our successes and failures is pretty constant. So, if you want more successes, you are going to have to tolerate more failures along the way.

If you are truly ready to change your game, your own unique learning experiences are resources of significant value and have already been customized for you as a result of your having lived them. Examining what you *already know* will enable you to understand what has worked in the past—and what hasn't—and enable you to get fresh results in the present. If you can move past any lingering denial, your past experiences are permanently available within you for evaluation and application to your challenges today. Creation requires learning from both success *and* failure and finding the personal power in all of it.

The willingness to write a failure resume in the form of a letter to one's children is a way to focus more on the "good learning" that resulted from past experiences, rather than on any negative outcomes, embarrassments or lost opportunities. This letter need not even be delivered (though if it is it could serve as a powerful example and perhaps an important lifeline). Delivered or not, it is a way to access a depth of self-assessment powerful enough to make a difference for you today.

* * *

If you are unable to celebrate and extract value from your subjective failures, you are ignoring a personal "power station" of knowledge—a resource with which you can increase the probability of your future successes.

* * *

Our learning experiences—no matter their outcomes at the time—are key parts of our uniqueness. In accessing them you access the unique *you* that will outperform others and enable you to take your game to new heights in the years ahead.

"We get the lives we get by the words we use."

As implied by this quote from Steve Chandler, author of *Time Warrior*, personal power begins in language. The words we use matter.[13] The first step is an understanding that words have *immense power* that can and should be harnessed in the creation of your plan for creating and managing your priorities. Your plan for changing your game is of necessity created in your own voice and through the

---

[13]Chandler, Steve. 2011. *Time Warrior: How to defeat procrastination, people-pleasing, self-doubt, over-commitment, broken promises and chaos.* Maurice Bassett.

specific words you select to bring your creation to life. Non-verbal communication, feelings and other methods of accessing your internal strengths and resources all have a role to play; but your own voice is the dominant factor in shaping your thoughts and actions.

Think of your choices of words and phrases as the fuel propelling you into action. Powerful words of clarity, intention and action have a much better chance of moving you in the direction of your desired outcomes. If you are choosing a proactive approach to daily living, doesn't it make sense to thoughtfully and carefully select the words that will maintain the appropriate velocity and cadence? The words we choose can bring real power to our process of creation and articulate the process of achieving what we desire.

Larry Wilson passed along to me this gem attributed to George Shapiro of the University of Minnesota: "The natural result of communication is misunderstanding." This is true whether you are communicating with others or with yourself. Why risk creating ambiguity or misunderstanding by being sloppy with the language you choose to represent your thinking, planning and actions? Strive to be clear and specific—first and foremost with yourself. As Zig Ziglar has said, "Don't become a wandering generality. Be a meaningful specific."

As you create your game plan, be conscious of selecting action words to reflect your intentions, objectives and priorities. There is power in active and descriptive words conveying clarity, motion, urgency and value.

Once you are happy with the words and language guiding your own actions, start thinking about the words you select to interact with others. These words need to begin in their worlds. Your listeners or readers should be able to visualize and feel the results that can be theirs if they choose to engage with you. You will want your language to clearly and unambiguously communicate the uniqueness of the resources, creativity and service you will bring to the task. It doesn't matter whether you are engaged in commercial business, caring for a home and family, service to a non-profit enterprise, being a student or anything else.

The creation of your future begins and lives in the words you use to describe your offering and the value you are creating with your precious time and energy. Get the initial ideas on paper, but then be highly aware of the words you choose to define your future. Take your time and carefully select each word as if it matters. It does.

Chapter 8

Fooled By Randomness, or Just Fooled?

Things always become obvious after the fact.
Nassim Nicholas Taleb

I am not a politician, an economist, part of the Wall Street crowd, a banker or a retirement planner, nor have I ever been accused of being a member of a right- or left-wing conspiracy (that I know of). I have never before written a book. The observations made here are simply offered from my point of view as a baby boomer whose sixtieth birthday has passed.

Like so many others, I had fooled myself into holding on to a belief in the perpetual stability of traditional American financial and governmental institutions and systems. I held on to that view even after substantial damage was done to my personal financial situation.

The time leading up to and including what became known as the Great Recession was marked for me by a reduction in income, plummeting home value and diminished savings and investments. These blows were accentuated by an untimely and costly divorce. Even in the face of this reality, for a time I continued to blindly trust those institutions that seemed so stable and reliable when I was growing up.

Federal Reserve chairman Alan Greenspan, who oc-cupied what was arguably the best seat in the house from which to anticipate a massive and systemic financial catas-trophe, acknowledged that he was fooled, too. In testimony before the U.S. Senate he said, "Those of us who looked to the self-interest of the lending institutions to protect share-holders' equity—myself especially—are in a state of shocked disbelief." Are you kidding me?

The Numbers Don't Lie

My initial goal for *Life Expectancy* was to convey to the reader as objectively as I could how an aging American boomer (with plenty of generational company) was impacted by the shift in once-reliable American institutions, and by the related, significant American economic destabilization. Something else then occurred that moved me to *actually write* this book rather than simply consider it. I was invited by *The Conference Board* (an organization which—among other things—provides information on leading economic indicators and the Consumer Confidence Index [CCI]) to give a speech at one of their national conferences. The speech was for the benefit of senior executives of some of the largest and best-known companies and consulting firms in the world. I was asked to speak on the future of executive compensation in the context of sustainability. I viewed it as a terrific forum for me to offer my thoughts about the link between longer-term business success and tangible commitments to the principles of sustainability.

During the course of my preparation I reviewed a large amount of current and historical economic and other data. It wasn't long before I was struck by the fact that most of the charts were indicating consistent, long-term negative trends.

The data that ideally would be trending upward (e.g., job creation, personal savings, housing starts, the economic value of an education, strength/value of the dollar, etc.) were trending downward. The data that ideally would be trending downward (e.g., personal credit balances, unemployment and jobless claims, healthcare costs, number of Americans living in poverty, etc.) were trending upward.

I reviewed several dozen different charts and found the trends to be consistently supportive of results contrary to the good. The magnitude of what Nassim Nicholas Taleb calls the "fragility quotient" in the economic underpinnings of our government and financial institutions was unmistakable and growing.[14] Notwithstanding the acceleration contributed by the events and abuses immediately preceding the so-called Great Recession, it is abundantly clear from a review of long-term trends that the American economic tide has been slowly ebbing for several decades. It is also quite clear that we are not rapidly moving through a short-term "bump" or "blip" (although bursts of false hope here and there may make it appear that the worst is over).

---

[14]Taleb's latest book is *Antifragility: How to Live in a World We Don't Understand*.

My evaluation of these trends was that of an American citizen who got interested in the *pictures* of what led to the decline in the economic vitality of our country—the charts and graphs that are readily and publicly available to everyone. I had no special access and was not provided with any inside information. Any American who cares to connect these dots can do so simply by paying attention to the colorful charts and graphs relating to economic news appearing in *USA Today* during almost any ninety-day period.

Financial Atrophy

It is unfair to lay all of the blame at the feet of government and financial institutions. Many of our individual financial strategies (if given much thought at all) have been flawed too.

Consider this: According to work done by the National Bureau of Economic Research (via an article at WSJ.com[15]), 22.2% of U.S. citizens when questioned replied that they were *probably unable* to come up with $2,000 within thirty days and 27.9% said they were *certainly unable* to do so. The NBER paper cited above also contained this point: "On a more concrete basis . . . $2,000 [is about] the cost of an auto transmission replacement."

It would be hard to argue that the inability of half of all Americans to readily access $2,000 within a month does

---

[15]Izzo, Phil. 2011. Nearly Half of Americans are 'Financially Fragile.' *The Wall Street Journal*, May 23, Real Time Economics section.

not equate to pervasive financial fragility in our citizenry across many socio-economic groups. This means that many American households have virtually no backup resources for surprises, emergencies or even relatively modest extra requirements. It is clear that tens of millions of Americans are not well positioned to fend for themselves.

By having a 20/20 view of your relative financial position, you have the opportunity to do something about it. With incomes under stress, a less reliable government in economic terms and more healthcare costs ahead, something has to change. If you have never before considered planning to take care of the majority of your budgetary requirements for the balance of your life, it should now become a priority. Your understanding of this reality will motivate the actions required to create your own safety net starting now.

Our World Has Changed

After considering these trends, I was led swiftly to the conclusion that for boomers and older Americans the remainder of our lives will likely be profoundly different from what we expected. Whether in terms of employment, opportunity for and value of savings, relative asset values, government support and entitlements, social programs, healthcare, family dynamics and more, our lives will be different in ways that we likely didn't anticipate even just a few years ago. At a minimum we are facing unwelcome uncertainty in the sufficiency and reliability of income for simple, basic needs in the years ahead.

This realization, however, can serve as a wakeup call that includes the possibility for life-changing action to address your personal requirements. It should be viewed as a timely call to action for each of us. Because of the starkness of the reality, the American economic malaise could in fact be the best thing that has happened to the boomer generation.

I fully appreciate that these conclusions are no longer news for many and that most of us have become a bit numb from the flood of reports confirming the fragile state of current and foreseeable American economic conditions.

I now believe that the personal impacts of the economic dislocation of the past several years will be far-reaching and lasting across all generations. Many of us have been or will eventually find ourselves in the middle of an unwelcome financial chasm—where the gap between our resources and our needs will be impossibly wide.

In the past we assumed, especially as boomer-Americans, that each generation's opportunities would enable a higher and better standard of living than the one before. This assumption has turned out to be false.

The Income Gap

As I put this through my sixty-year-old filter of "What does this mean for me?" it became crystal clear that the economic circumstances ahead for me—and for the huge population of forty-five-plus year-olds heading into what have traditionally been known as *retirement years*—could be quite challenging.

There will be a significant shortfall between the quality of the retirement years we have anticipated and what will actually be the case if we do not take action to close it. The challenge of closing this gap will be a stretch for TENS OF MILLIONS OF AMERICANS. Many boomers have not yet fully realized the gap exists, let alone started planning for and acting upon what needs to be done to address it.

There are plenty of people writing and talking about what all of the data and information means in terms of government and financial institution health, Social Security, Medicare, and future economic conditions. For Americans forty-five and older, it doesn't much matter what anyone writes or tells us about why it may get better (temporarily or in the long term) or why we should hold out hope for the future.

In the form of a silver lining in the aftermath of the storm of the Great Recession, I discovered for myself the heart of the formula for game-changing action. Although I had been fooled, I was able to begin the creation of a powerful new incarnation that leveraged my uniqueness in the service of those for whom I could be of greatest value. My creation was not based on an approach unique to me. It wasn't an accident and it wasn't luck. In fact, you can use the same basic formula yourself to change your own game. Your age today simply doesn't matter.

Chapter 9

"Protect Yourself at All Times!"

Reward is always relative to risk. If any product or invest-
ment sounds like it has lots of upside,
it also has lots of risk.
Barry Ritholtz

Too few Americans now do a sufficient amount of work for long enough periods during their lives.

This labor insufficiency is a serious structural problem that has been decades in the making. We have thirty-year-old students and fifty-year-old retirees (and a lot of unemployed people) and then wonder why the minimalist remains of the working population in between can't make the math add up. In 1950 there were about 16.5 contributors for each person receiving Social Security benefits and the average life expectancy was about sixty-eight. It worked. Today, there are about three contributors for each recipient and the average life expectancy is around seventy-eight. It doesn't work. It can't work. And it isn't going to get better any time soon.

According to data published by the U.S. Census Bu-
reau, at the time of this writing over forty-six million Amer-
icans live below the poverty line. Another ninety-seven million Americans fall into the low-income category (com-

monly defined as those earning between 100 and 199 percent of poverty level) based on a supplemental measure provided by the Census Bureau. This means that *the number of Americans who are poor or low-income is approximately 146 million*—roughly forty-eight percent of the U.S. population.

All indications are that this number will rise. This means that a significant portion of the American population is paying little income tax into government coffers (or into retirement accounts) and now or eventually will require more supplemental aid from all sources. The default answer has historically been to look for more support from our government. Unfortunately today this does not appear to be a realistic option for a government that is already borrowing approximately forty-one cents of every dollar it spends. (This borrowing is driving additional national debt by over two million dollars *every single minute*, twenty-four-hours of every day.)

By most practical definitions our federal government is bankrupt. You cannot reasonably expect it to do what it has promised generations of American voters it would do when we got old, or to act for those who have requirements that have traditionally been fulfilled through government programs.

The good news is that because of the accumulation of wave after wave of sobering facts we can now see what is real. In some ways it is like the discovery of an elephant that has been with us in the room all along. Once the truth is revealed—no matter how seemingly difficult—it bursts the bubble of hope that we might have attached to it. Clarity relieves us of any lingering attachment to procrastination as a coping strategy. It encourages right actions, right now.

For example, please don't dream about receiving a Social Security check to cover for the fact that over the past forty or fifty years you didn't save enough money for retirement. This traditional form of payback for a lifetime of work and contributions is an income source for aging Americans (and others who are eligible) that could well disappear during this decade or the next. Though it is not your fault individually that we have had political leadership for decades that hasn't run the government as a business, it *is* now your problem.

Trust in Thee

Given the many variables in the economic environment, putting your money and faith in things you truly understand is the surest way to keep what you have—even if it doesn't grow or create a return. Doing so in this environment reminds me of the number one boxing instruction: "Protect yourself at all times when you're in the ring."

Anything else is *investment as gambling*, with "unlucky" as the most probable outcome. There are many good, detailed analyses of what occurred to irrevocably change the post-Great Recession world, but I recommend two: The HBO movie *Too Big to Fail*, and the documentary *Inside Job*.[16]

---

[16]*Too Big to Fail*. Directed by Curtis Hanson. 2011; Santa Monica, CA, HBO Films. *Inside Job*. Directed by Charles Ferguson. 2010; Culver City: CA, Sony Pictures Classics.

Both make clear that the financial markets are never, ever an even playing field for individuals.

There was a time when an average investor, if asked, "Where do you invest your money?" might have proudly answered: "I am invested in the stock market; I'm making money with the big boys on Wall Street." It is unsurprising that the big boys have always had the house advantage, rendering the *making money* part of the equation very uncertain for you.

Wall Street professionals have always had the advantage of *asymmetrical information*. This is one of Barry Ritholtz's 15 Inviolable Rules for Dealing with Wall Street.[17] This advantage favors the party to a negotiated sale that is in possession of more information, knowledge and data about the product being bought and sold than the *other party*. In the case of Wall Street trading the other party will almost always be *you*.

There are forces at work on Wall Street that even the sophisticated professional players in the game don't fully understand. Consider that something close to seventy percent of stock trades on the *New York Stock Exchange* are initiated and completed by software programs running complex algorithms. The speed of this buying and selling is mind-boggling and sometimes results in a share of stock

---

[17]Ritholtz, Barry. 2010. 15 Inviolable Rules for Dealing with Wall Street. <http://www.ritholtz.com/blog/2010/10/15-inviolable-rules-for-dealing-with-wall-street/> For more about Mr. Ritholz, see <http://www.ritholtz.com/blog/barry-ritholtz-curriculum-vitae/>

being owned for mere milliseconds. None of these kinds of rapid transactions are being made by your neighbor sitting at his kitchen table. It is sophisticated, very high speed, program trading. You might say it is trading untouched by human hands.

And if you expected plain language explanations from the financial leadership in our country, guess again. The dialect that is spoken by them can be like an exotic foreign language only understood by the locals. On one average day the chairman of the Federal Reserve Board, Ben Bernanke, made the comment, "The possibility remains that the recent economic weakness may prove more persistent than expected, and the deflationary risks might reemerge, implying a need for additional policy support."

Yes, that is an actual quote.

The truth of the matter is that really smart individual investors have only casino odds of being successful over the long term in the market for equities.

In terms of protecting yourself in the economic and financial environment we will live with for the next several decades, I submit that *real* people have to rely upon being part of the *real* economy creating *real* jobs and *real* value to create a future that is *real*. In this state of *reality* there is much less ambiguity; the risks are more obvious and therefore—in many cases—more manageable.

Trusted Representatives

When the financial institutions were getting bailed out there was virtually no help for people who couldn't pay their mortgages. There was a total lack of urgency displayed by our elected representatives. There was no relief for average Americans, leading to tremendous stresses and uncertainty for millions of families. If you were expecting to be protected, it was another case of disappointment.

If *ever* there was an opportunity for our political leadership to act in the service of its constituents and *do something of real and immediate value*—it was then. It didn't happen. There wasn't any real advocacy for programs or policies that would enable people to keep their homes—the outward manifestation of the now *old* American dream.

If our elected representatives would not (or could not) stand up to be counted with a real solution for Americans at that crucial juncture, how can we possibly trust that it will be any different in the future? Please don't. Please don't be naïve by harboring such hopes at the expense of your own self-reliant action.

I am not suggesting that the financial bailouts for the largest pillars of our financial infrastructure were inappropriate—clearly something had to be done. But it was simply wrong to leave the individual American citizen out of the equation. In my view this failure to act with the required urgency was the height of arrogance, recklessness and neglect by our elected representatives.

It was a moment for powerful leadership in the service of American citizens that passed with barely a whimper.

The Kindness of Strangers

Though they market themselves as being in your corner, many brokers, bankers and financial planners more closely resemble parasites than trusted advisors. They don't have any answers for you either. They can't. You really can't blame them for working to persuade you to continue creating income for them by keeping you in the same old dead ends they have always had in their bags. Most are not personally invested in you other than as a source of fee income, and virtually none of them are willing or able to think outside the box of history. And their history is populated by examples of their miserable failures to even minimally protect the source of their personal and corporate largesse: the borrowing and investing public.

In the continuing wake of economic stresses it is unsurprising that there are more and more financial sharks in the water looking for blood in the form of whatever assets you may still have. The North American Securities Administrators Association is a group of state securities regulators. They have reported a recent doubling in the number of cases involving investment fraud targeted against baby boomers. And these only represent the cases where personal embarrassment has been sufficiently overcome to report the fraud. There are likely many more.

* * *

I can imagine that right about now you may be feeling a bit depressed, which is understandable. I offer the somewhat bleak points above to illustrate the importance of realizing that your money must now be your own for preservation and protection.

* * *

The plans for boomers to create a future addressing their basic needs must have a greater element of self-reliance than we could have imagined even just a few years ago. It is a time for caution, and for remembering that "Reward is always relative to risk."

As you think about the cash flow part of your plan for the rest of your life I suggest focusing on that which you have the possibility of understanding and controlling by virtue of your own commitment and actions. Your power is in financial conservatism—even frugality. You will need to recapture that power in order to enable the creation that is the remainder of your life. The rest is simply trouble.

Chapter 10

Here Lies Retirement: R.I.P.

*We live in a moment of history where change
is so speeded up that we begin to see the present
only when it is already disappearing.*
R. D. Laing

Retirement was once considered the golden twilight of the traditional American life cycle at its most linear, benign and comfortable. But traditional retirement no longer works in our society. In reality it hasn't worked for a long time. We just haven't gotten around to creating a new version to take its place.

Why doesn't it work? As mentioned earlier, in the 1950s, the average retirement age was sixty-five and the average life expectancy was about sixty-eight. Resources were available to match the requirements for living. Age mile-posted cookie-cutter traditional retirement is no longer a match for generations that will live to an average age range of seventy-seven to eighty-five. For individuals today who are fifty or fifty-five or sixty years of age, a large percentage of life remains—decades for most. And it takes money to live even a modest life over so many years.

Traditional retirement has also had a weird irony associated with it: the removal of highly experienced workers—many of whom may be at the top of their games—from positions where they might very well have had the opportunity to make significant, continuing contributions for businesses and institutions that really need them.

Very capable people have been prematurely forced out to make way for a new generation of workers who are less experienced, possibly less valuable and perhaps possessing a less well-developed work ethic. In some cases the new workers are more interested in what they can *get* from an employment situation rather than making sure they are delivering *service* that will make them worthy of retention.

Aging Americans have nonetheless continued to anticipate that now lengthier periods of retirement driven by increasing life expectancies will be fully paid for by ever-appreciating homes, the value of rising stock portfolios and savings, and by a little payback from decades of contributions to the Social Security system and other retirement accounts. However, just as the first boomers were approaching the age of sixty-five, the anticipated rewards and long-expected entitlements of a slowed down "good life" were upended.

An American economic malaise—unexpected by many—has impacted and is still impacting home acquisition, ownership and retention, as well as employment, social programs and opportunities, family stability, healthcare and virtually every other aspect of American life. For most boomers of working or retirement age, this condition is unfolding as a very personal story of shrinking personal asset values just when they are needed to take us further than ever before. It has already affected—in some cases severely—the lifestyles and well-being of those *currently* retired and of many other Americans with limited or fixed incomes.

Creative Destruction

The truth of the matter is that traditional retirement is off the table for many Americans. The arrival of this at first unwelcome new reality may signal the overdue meltdown of an economic model that has outlived its usefulness. Consider it a form of creative destruction—meaning the creation, through asset devaluation, of an opportunity to build something new where the old has crumbled. According to its Wikipedia entry, creative destruction can be characterized as the process whereby "capitalism destroys and reconfigures previous economic orders . . . It must ceaselessly devalue existing wealth (whether through war, dereliction, or regular and periodic economic crises) in order to clear the ground for the creation of new wealth." A more common example of creative destruction is the process known as "downsizing," whereby a business reduces its number of employees in order to improve the efficiency and profitability of the company.

A very good argument can be made that this process of *clearing away what no longer works* has been taking place in America over the past several years (or maybe even more gradually over prior decades.) Consider it a somewhat extreme, but timely and fortuitous, wake-up call. It is not too late to respond to it through action.

Aging in the Mainstream

Whether you agree or not with the concept of creative destruction as a force serving periodic economic renewal, it is obvious that we stand at a crossroads in history where we must shift from the old concept of retirement to a new one I will call *aging in the mainstream.*

The paradigms of employment, retirement, home ownership and a youth-driven culture are all under revision. This shift represents an exciting opportunity for boomers to remain an active presence in the mainstream. Transitioning into this new form of (non-)retirement can be as fresh and dynamic an experience as graduating from high school or college and first entering the workforce may have been for you. You may decide, among other things, to start a new business of your own for the first time (as an *elderpreneur*), or to change careers to do something you always thought you would have more fun at—or even *love* to do.

* * *

The present need not represent what was lost or diminished, or what failed us. It can represent the starting point for the most powerful period of our lives. It can be a time when we use our individual talents and experience and wisdom to our best advantage and serve others in the process.

* * *

It doesn't matter that many of us might *have to do this* in order to earn income to cover basic needs or to supplement savings and other assets. There is no reason to see the situation as a loss of the *right* to retire. Retirement never was a right (and in my opinion it was overrated as a way of moving through the remaining years of living). There is every reason to stay involved in a societal mainstream that is faster and more vibrant and interesting than ever before. The disappearance of traditional retirement may actually enhance the quality of the boomers' later years.

But there is also a financial reality that must be addressed. Let me ask you a simple question. Who or what do you now expect to care for you in economic terms when you are an elderly person? What will you do if you have a heart attack or get cancer or become disabled? These things are much more likely to occur as we get older. Healthcare is a mess and costs are ever increasing as a percentage of fixed incomes.

It does not appear likely that the younger generations can be counted on to take care of *themselves*, let alone their parents—even if they want to do so. They too will have to deal with change at an ever-increasing rate, and they will have their own issues—financial and otherwise—to deal with.

For many of us there is little room for error in the years ahead. The natural order of work followed by retirement and a calculated transition out of the work force is not a viable option for a good portion of the boomer population. Ongoing productive contributions must now replace the slower pace previously enjoyed by people approaching and passing the age of retirement.

For some, the relative calm with which they have viewed advancing age (and its once promising freedom) has been replaced with anger at the patent unfairness of the country's financial situation, its timing and the personal and family destabilization it has wrought. However, we cannot remain stunned or angry for too long or we will get run over by the American generations following ours, as well as by the generations of citizens around the world that we have helped to economically enable.

If the traditional world of a retirement more-or-less outside of the mainstream of work life and economic activity is ever restored, it will take—at a minimum—several generations, perhaps even longer. It will also require massive and painful changes by governments, institutions, businesses large and small, and individuals rich and poor. The degree and period of cooperation that will be required among these constituencies virtually dooms the task before it has begun. Assuming complete cooperation from all constituent interests, restoration of previous levels of economic security will also take an enormous measure of luck.

Older for Longer

The good news is that the average life expectancy in America continues to lengthen. For many, health care advancements enable high quality, energetic living for a lot of years after sixty-five. But as a society we *cannot afford* to take experienced, productive resources and put them on the bench simply because of their date stamp.

When I say "cannot afford," I mean that we cannot afford to lose the contributions these workers make, but also that it is simply no longer financially tenable for our government to assume the role of primary provider of their income, housing or health care—not for three or five years or even seven years, but for up to twenty years. The math doesn't work. The solution has to be different.

The shift from traditional retirement to the new paradigm is well underway, though many are still in denial—afraid to look at the reality ahead. Just because it is different than traditional off-the-grid retirement doesn't mean that aging in the mainstream has to be drudgery.

You can choose to downshift the speed at which you operate if you want to. You can create a more flexible or even home-based work style. You can choose to be your own boss. You can harness your hobbies in the service of income. You can enter partnerships you had always thought about. You can energetically fill the days and years ahead as determined by you, your experience, your uniqueness, your desires *and* your financial requirements. You can pursue whatever you can envision. This is the essence of changing your game for the rest of your life. Awareness of your mortality and economic self-interest can be your motivational muses.

Our World Has Changed

The main goal I have in writing *Life Expectancy* is to raise the awareness of aging boomers and other older Americans about what are likely to be very personal life challenges ahead, and to encourage proactive preparation for them.

The first and easiest approach to the realization of economic adversity is almost always denial and rationalization. Your first thought may be why this situation will not be true in your specific case. And perhaps it will not be. There are Americans who have indeed "saved for a rainy day"; they are proof positive of the power of self-reliance, planning and fiscal responsibility. If the examination of your own situation objectively leads to the conclusion that you already possess or can access the resources needed to be comfortable for the rest of your life, congratulations are in order. Please continue on your way and enjoy the rest of your life with the ease and peace that will be yours with no financial pressures.

I do not believe this will be true for the majority of aging Americans.

The erosion of the long-trusted fundamental underpinnings of our economy—including governmental and financial institutions—will have lasting and mostly deleterious effects on individual earning capacities, opportunities, wherewithal and financial support programs for most Americans. And frankly, these adverse conditions will now apply to *almost all Americans* no matter their ages.

The same financial ingenuity and opportunism that were the major catalysts for the financial meltdown immediately precipitating the Great Recession will eventually power our economy out of its financial malaise (and make rich another generation of creative financiers). But in the meantime, as the bulge population of boomers has begun turning sixty-five and older, Americans are facing very practical and long-term economic challenges that must be addressed and managed.

Creating the Rest of Your Life

Fortunately, the sky is not *actually* falling. We shouldn't be—and I am not—pessimistic about the viability of our country or its current and future position of leadership in the world. But with tens of millions of Americans approaching the same intersection, to the quick and the adaptable will go the advantages.

A hallmark of youth is flexibility—the ability to quickly adapt to changing circumstances by virtue of not having opinions and thinking processes that are in a state of *rigor mortis*. Older Americans can adopt this type of flexibility as well, but it will take a conscious, ongoing effort to challenge our thinking and ensure that it is continuously informed by the facts of today's world. It will require the generation of energy that we might rather have spent in the direction of something less critical to our well-being.

In order to access and create that energy, we need to do some things we may not have done for a long time. We need to grow from the inside out, to spread our branches and feel the breeze. Go outside and breathe the air, sit on a boulder in the sun, lie in the grass, listen to the wind in the trees. Take the time to look at the stars and the clouds, to sit outside for an hour in the middle of the night, to listen to the quiet offered by a new blanket of snow. All of these things and more can provide needed *space* for your creative mind to generate and engage the energy for creating the rest of your life.

* * *

I am much more optimistic that we can make our way by initiating powerful change at the individual rather than the institutional or governmental level.

* * *

As individuals, the kind of personal change required will include a revision of longstanding (and probably unchallenged) beliefs to comport more closely with the reality of the rapidly evolving environment and more complex requirements of today. We must now shift our game of the past to make it viable for our future.

As each of us approaches and passes the traditional

age of retirement, there is an opportunity to examine our lives and circumstances in order to create a proactive and thoughtful future. Insight into the scarcity of our time and financial resources can be a great motivator for change. Scarcity creates value. The remainder of our lives is precious—priceless, in fact.

Our life planning must include the prioritization of what we choose to do and be, to whom and what we choose to commit, limit or avoid. The question each of us must answer is, "How will I consciously select the priorities for each of the remaining days of my life?" Consistently wrestling with these issues may be a challenge, but it is worth doing; it can turn our daily routine into a daily adventure.

We have received a timely, generational wake-up call signaling that we must remain in the mainstream of society and continue earning income for much or all of the remainder of our lives. It is now and will continue to be uncomfortable, but at the same time it is a situation filled with potential. There is an excitement in this reframing of aging that can be amazingly energizing. Even if you have been on the bench for decades, now could be the moment to say, "Put me in coach, I'm ready to play." Only in this instance, you act as both coach *and* player.

It is a great time to embrace game-changing thinking to *create* the rest of our lives through active, personal choices. The cavalry is not coming to the rescue—unless you are prepared for the cavalry to be you.

Chapter 11

The Power Generation

*Why should we stunt our ambitions and impoverish our
lives in order to be insulted and looked down upon
in our old age?*
Joseph A. Schumpeter

If you are over the age of forty-five, it is quite likely
you have been underestimated in some fashion. Our society
has traditionally favored the young over the old. This preference has not caused much of a problem, until now.

The traditionally accepted linear progression of life in
the past fifty years has worked for most of us from birth to
death. We have more or less accepted our roles at each stage:
infant, kid, the student years of teenager, young adult, and
the early twenties, the working years and parenthood, leading into middle age, grandparenthood, retirement, and
finally the elderly years.

These are labels that have worked well enough to
comfortably pigeonhole us as we have moved through the
passages of life. Older always giving way to younger. Parents
moving out of the way so that children can themselves grow
into the parental role and deliver grandchildren. Grandparents moving out of the mainstream workforce and into

retirement communities. Elderly Americans quietly fading into invisibility and finally into dust.

In some societies, elders are revered for their experience, wisdom and advice; younger people look up to them and expect to care for their senior family members in their later years. Such respect and care is viewed not only as a responsibility but as a privilege. It also foreshadows the transitions the younger caregivers will undergo as they age and ultimately require care themselves.

In the U.S., many younger people are dismissive of aging members of society. "What could you possibly know— you're old and slow. Get outta my way. Make way for *meeeeeeeee*." Their view is that aging Americans are irrelevant or even offensive. They exhibit an attitude that portrays older people as burdensome in a society that has long celebrated youth as panacea.

Some of the apparent derision is not only without malice, it is purely a function of youthful bravado, inexperience and to some degree playing an age-appropriate societal role. In any event, there is no reason to ignore, marginalize or take advantage of any age group or other population segment in favor of aging Americans. A healthy society necessarily has constructive tension and legitimate advocacy for people of all ages. However, in my view, older Americans have traditionally not been as forceful in being heard as circumstances now dictate.

We have the opportunity to embrace different expectations for ourselves and to lead the way for the generations following ours. Most of us do not have the benefit of savings that can cover us for the rest of our lives—not even close. We have suffered significant losses on investments in the stock market. Other investments designed to create retirement income and to pay for some of the increasing costs of health care have been losing propositions, eating away at our precious nest eggs. There may be little or no equity in our homes, which have for generations been principal sources of basic comfort in retirement. For some, our homes have morphed into cash-eating albatrosses wrapped around our necks—ones we have no choice but to continue feeding.

The Greatest (Potential) Voting Coalition in History

Today in the U.S. there are about forty million Americans over the age of sixty-five. By 2020 this number gets close to fifty-five million, and by 2030 it will exceed seventy million. By 2040, it is expected there will be about eighty million people in the U.S. age sixty-five and older. EIGHTY MILLION! This also means there will be eighty million potential *voters* over the age of sixty-five, a good portion of who may actually take the time to go to the polls for a *good cause*, rain or shine. Solving the then-certain societal and economic aging issues will certainly qualify as a good cause.

This is not just a rising, abstract trend. This is a fundamental power shift in the fabric of American society. The idea of embracing and harnessing this power hasn't yet reached our generation's collective consciousness. But the time has come. The oft-quoted movie line takes on a more urgent reality: "We're mad as hell and we're not going to take it anymore." When there are tens of millions of us, the concept of *not taking it anymore* can be more than a mere idle threat.

If you are over forty-five today, you could be a part of what has the potential to be *the greatest voting coalition in the history of the world.* If properly developed and managed, the agenda, interests and requirements of the elders in our society can trump those of any other demographic coalition. For at least the next thirty years, the needs and desires of this potential voting bloc will have to be represented front and center by politicians who "get it."

The power of the boomer generation has been there all along, but it has never been consolidated as a force for generational self-interest. If there is urgency around the shifts needed to support non-retirement-based aging (or aging in the mainstream), this latent power can be brought to bear in the creation of real solutions.

To tap into that collective power, it will take a purposeful effort at the individual level to exercise our brains, stay curious, change the routine, learn some new things, read something different, embrace technology, go to lectures, see movies at theaters instead of from the couch, visit university campuses, take a class in anything... The trick is to break out of whatever stagnation may have crept into your life. You are the expert in what will work for you to keep yourself in the mainstream of *thinking* and *doing* as you get older.

* * *

I can envision the creation of a pragmatic and apolitical platform to make clear the as yet unaddressed requirements of the boomer generation—accompanied by a significant level of noise and fury given that the moment of need is at hand.

* * *

Armed with this platform as a roadmap we will have at least a fighting chance for getting things done by electing politicians who understand and are supportive of the needs of aging Americans.

The paradigm of older as weaker, less vital, expendable, invisible, second-class or less important is *wrong*. Boomers must not accept this outmoded view as their reality. We must recognize that such an assessment is based on traditional roles and outdated thinking. Instead of allowing ourselves to be kicked around and pandered to because we are older, we can now stand up and fend for ourselves. Rather than allowing politicians to sell us a false vision of the old retirement, encouraging us to recede into that state of passive acceptance, we can put people in office who understand the new non-retirement and who will help us thrive.

Power Shift

This fundamental shift is now possible. Youth has always loudly proclaimed its advantages. But we must stake our claim to the advantages of having lived longer, of having seen and experienced more. There is no reason to accept being turned out to pasture—and we can't afford to do it. *Nowhere is it written that aging must be unpleasant, isolating, marginalizing and sedentary.*

You don't have to go there if you can commit to making the rest of your life different than you may have expected it to be and can see the richness available in aging in the mainstream of American society. We cannot remain on the sidelines. In fact, those boomers who stay on the sidelines longest will have the fewest opportunities and will likely end up the most disadvantaged.

The fact is that as the road ahead gets shorter for aging boomers and other Americans, everything will be magnified. Health issues, economic challenges and age-related discrimination are among the stresses. Being younger typically means better health, more time to recover from mistakes, and the option to be a little less urgent about the daily creation and commitments that make for a purposefully meaningful life (though I wouldn't consider the latter point a best practice at any age.)

Whatever can be driven now to address the impact of the ebbing of the American economic condition for boomers will ultimately benefit all Americans—no matter their current ages. The metronome of life sounds for all at the same rate, no matter the individual point in our passages. The twenty-year-old of today becomes the forty-year-old of tomorrow. The forty-year-old becomes the eighty-year old.

As boomers, there is real power in our numbers, our voices, our buying power and our voting influence. We are consumers, opinion leaders, grassroots activists and thinking people. We are not distracted by teen romance, the latest clothing trends, testosterone and acne-fueled angst, getting through high school and college or starting families.

We are fully baked and ready for action. We are serious-minded and don't expect to be offered do-overs just because we are fine young men and women. There are certainly advantages to being younger, but those advantages can fade as quickly as the arrival of that first gray hair or wrinkle, that first, mysterious "extra five pounds."

We can envision a society where younger generations of workers will have to win their places through their own brand of old-fashioned self-reliance and initiative. While serving our own interests we will also be showing them ways to be self-reliant and productive. We can lead by example.

We can commit to the mainstream of life for the rest of our days rather than peacefully going off to the back roads and byways, out of sight and earshot and mind. Instead of collapsing into passive retirement, we can try our damnedest, using all of our hard-earned experience and ability, to stay in our jobs as long as we can contribute.

And I don't mean staying through the old preordained retirement age of sixty-two or sixty-five. We will now work through and after seventy, maybe until seventy-five or eighty. Then maybe we will work part-time for the rest of our days. How about *them* apples!

Rather than seeing this as a tragedy, it could be the very blessing we've been looking for to put this country back on the road to recovery and renewed prosperity. The continuation of positive boomer contributions in the mainstream can benefit all generations following ours. Our commitment to self-reliance will produce income, jobs and asset value for others. As might have been said in the 1960s, "It can be an epic time, man." Individually and collectively there is a lot of power remaining in the boomer generation—maybe more than ever before.

Growing Up

In *The Next Decade: Empire and Republic in a Changing World*, George Friedman writes that four things are needed to "develop the culture and institutions needed to manage (our) republic cast in an imperial role."

> First, a nation that has an unsentimental understanding of the situation it is in. Second, leaders who are prepared to bear the burden of reconciling that reality with American values. Third, presidents who understand power and principles and know the place of each. But above all, what is needed is a mature American public that recognizes what is

at stake and how little time there is...[18]

Although these points at first may seem to stray a bit from the themes of *Life Expectancy*, I suggest that these elements *applied to our individual circumstances* are of equal import and could illuminate the path for changing your future outcomes. By way of analogy, I suggest that as aging Americans we first must have an *unsentimental and objective understanding of our individual challenges*. Without this, any decisions we make about our individual directions and priorities will be flawed from the start.

Second, at a personal level *we must reconcile any gap between our current activity and what is required of us* to step up to a greater level of self-reliance.

Third, we must *connect as individuals to the national agenda* by voting for representatives who best serve our needs and who will create a climate that allows our entrepreneurial spirit to thrive.

Finally, we must recognize that our ability to change our own circumstances requires an *emotional maturity and clarity* that we may not have yet reached, despite our chronological years.

How many times have you observed people behaving as though they have the mentality of college (or even high school) students, although several decades have passed since

---

[18]Friedman, George. 2012. *The Next Decade: Empire and Republic in a Changing World*. New York: Random House. Friedman is also the author of *The Next 100 Years: A Forecast for the 21st Century.*

they left campus life? Given what is at stake for each of us and how little time there is to select and implement our choices, we need to embrace a greater level of maturity *now*.

The time has come for a new, purposeful, focused and committed voting coalition based upon our common and serious economic interests. We will need boomer leaders to help us create the grassroots infrastructure and systems to properly harness and direct this massive generational power. Our platform must address both common- and self-interests. These interests will have to be blended and balanced in order to provide both collective and individual value for our generation and for those that follow it.

If we rise to the task we will have an unprecedented opportunity to rebuild the foundation of American society at a time when it is more necessary to do so than at any prior moment in our lifetimes. We can turn this country around, individually and collectively.

* * *

We can lead a return to self-reliance, frugality, civility, fairness, straight talk, commitment, entrepreneurship, job creation and other values and characteristics that once defined the American way of life.

* * *

We could see aging Americans deliver a reprise of self-reliance, independent thinking and capitalism. The values that once shaped American life could become some of the platform planks supporting a return to *apolitical economic sanity* for all generations of Americans for the next thirty or forty years—which might be long enough to restore vibrancy to our economic foundation. Given our domestic challenges and the shifting global landscape, it would be much preferable that the course ahead no longer be about political agendas. Although I perfectly understand that this vision may sound pollyannaish, I believe that—in our best interests—we must demand the development and delivery of tangible, practical results for ordinary American citizens.

Boomers can and should demand politics and progress for the common good. Given the enormous latent generational power at our disposal, this will be an important step in the direction of the revitalization of our democratic republic in the form that was for so long the envy of the world. In this, there is the opportunity for both a lasting generational legacy and individual, high-performance aging in the mainstream.

Chapter 12

Musical Chairs

I hate being young, but I don't want to be old.
Anonymous

In many ways *all* generations are in the midst of a perfect storm of unanticipated economic adversity and societal upheaval. The economic dislocation witnessed over the past several years is ongoing, and it could have an even greater impact on younger generations—those made up of individuals below forty-five years of age—than on boomers and post-retirement-age citizens. These include Generations X, Y and Z (for simplicity, I will hereafter refer to all of them as the "*Alphabets*").

Whatever else boomers may have done or not done, they have mastered the free enterprise system as a means for feeding their appetites for material things. Although many boomers have depleted their savings and suffered significant declines in asset value over the past few years (and have borrowed and repaid substantial amounts of consumer credit), they have a generational aptitude for creating new businesses (from lemonade stands in youth to software companies as adults) and for entrepreneurship in general.

Boomers have subsidized some of the Alphabets to the

point where a perception has been created that starting a business or developing a strong work ethic is unnecessary, that it is something not expected of them. In fact, some Alphabets have become rock throwers against the free market system and openly supportive of alternative means of advancement. (There are also, of course, current examples of spectacularly successful young entrepreneurs.)

* * *

The concept of declining relevance due to aging is a lie that our society can no longer tolerate. A new form of generational competition has the potential for ending like a game of musical chairs—without a chair for everyone. We have no choice but to accept the challenge and play the game to its conclusion.

* * *

Frankly, we must push this agenda in order to assure our economic relevance as individuals. We cannot accept being marginalized as a function of chronological age. We have to reframe our thinking to view our age and experience as assets (which they clearly are) to be leveraged in our service and in the service of those around us.

Gray Power

Boomers must now embrace the fortunate truth that there is no automatic deficit that arrives at forty-five, fifty-five or sixty-five. No matter what you may *think* you see in the lines on your face, and no matter what you *feel* when you start moving your body in the morning, the essence of you is now at its best. The advantages that older Americans possess as a result of experiencing years of life simply cannot be reached through short-cuts. By definition this advantage cannot go to youth.

Tens of millions of younger potential competitors for jobs, entrepreneurial opportunities, roles requiring thoughtful decision-making and more, are disadvantaged because they don't have what boomers have. It can't be bought with anything but the passage of years. This life experience represents individual and collective strength that we must leverage to our advantage.

Economic necessity for aging boomers must now overrule the old parental mantra of, "Our role in life is to make it easier for our children." Many of us as parents have said, "I want my daughter or son to have the advantages I didn't have," and have made the road for our children as smooth as possible, sometimes subordinating our own requirements and desires along the way. That's what parents were *supposed* to do.

And now many of us have grown or almost grown children who must become self-reliant in their own right. Although it may appear selfish on our part to help this process along, it truly is a matter of serving their best interests. At one point in her college career I stopped paying my daughter Natalie's tuition because I felt that I had much more interest (financial and otherwise) in her education at that point than she did. After a year or so away from campus (in the fast food industry), she determined she could be interested after all, and was a willing scholar from then through graduation.

Continuing to act as parental *safety nets* for all the bumps in the road has a potential unintended consequence: undermining the development of the independence and self-reliance critical to our children's success in meeting their own life challenges. Instead of this, I believe we will hear more boomer parents and grandparents say, "You're on your own."

Boomers are now dealing with the self-interest of necessity, which doesn't include much room for long-term subsidies for children (no matter how terrific they may be). Simply put, given the economic pressures on individuals forty-five years and older, the Alphabets (including those in your own family) will see a lot of Gray Power in the work force for a lot longer. These older workers are in many ways better equipped with education, verbal communication skills, experience and expertise learned on the job than are the Alphabets. The forty-five and older crowd is prepared to compete to keep places in the work force—and they are serious about it. They will do battle to keep their income streams alive. If that means continuing to occupy a spot that might once have gone to a younger person—or even replacing a younger worker—so be it.

Today's game is about self-sufficiency and *doing what you have to do* to create a way forward. There will be no making room just because the person competing against you is young enough to be your own child—or even grandchild.

"Let Me Give that Some Thought..."

Another advantage for the forty-five-plus year old generations is that they have not been as heavily impacted as the Alphabets by the distractions of the internet. Social media networks and entertainment sites like Facebook, Twitter, Tumblr, YouTube and others certainly have their places, but they can also serve to continuously interrupt the steady flow of a workday and consume huge chunks of leisure time available for other creative pursuits. The effects of sound bites, texting and a steady stream of bits and bytes of all kinds, have turned several generations into perpetually digitally attached, reactive responders.

The good news for boomers is that for younger people, social network peer pressure is at an all-time high due to the ubiquity of life experienced in photos, sounds, music, video and more—all online, in real time and with little left to the imagination. The under-forty-fives must spend substantial time and effort staying plugged in to these networks lest they be left out of something or left behind.

Distractions like these provide potential advantages for older Americans. Many boomers have better developed abilities to deal with tasks that require reflection, reasoning and aptitude, and which may take more than a few minutes (or seconds!) of concentration.

Self-Reliance at Every Age

If you see value in these points and are concerned about the future for your kids, how do you respond to someone who asks, "How should I prepare for economic survival in forty years' time?"

Here's what I would say: "Frankly, if you are twenty-five (or even forty) and consider the disruptive changes that can be seen all around you, it is not too soon to get serious about what you will do to take care of yourself when you turn sixty-five. I've got news for most of you: Your parents are leaving you nothing. They won't be able to do so even if they want to, because by the time they pass away they will likely have spent every dollar they have and perhaps more."

I would add: "We have entered a new age of economic caution. I can tell you with certainty that the only absolutely viable answer is looking back at you in the mirror. No matter your age, the answer lies in your willingness to live each day with an unwavering commitment to independence, creativity and self-reliance from this day forward."

As parents, the best legacy we can provide is showing our children the way to become mature, self-sufficient adults. This is a gift that will keep on giving, and is perhaps the next best thing to leaving them millions (if we could). In the long run it might even be better.

Chapter 13

Choosing Ownership

People don't want their lives fixed. Nobody wants their problems solved. Their dramas. Their distractions. Their stories resolved. Their messes cleaned up. Because what would they have left? Just the big scary unknown.
Chuck Palahniuk[19]

Since you are the best, and really only, person with the means to take charge of the remainder of your life, choosing the healthiest of perspectives for yourself is the optimal starting point.

In business there is a simplistic way of characterizing virtually everyone you encounter: as a "deal maker" or a "deal killer." This may initially appear too simple a way of labeling what a person might objectively represent. But there is a design to the distinction that is pretty compelling. Deal makers are positive, looking for ways to move forward, eliminate barriers and engage in productive dialogue. They have a bias for problem resolution. Deal makers are aware of where the beginning was and where the finish line is supposed to be. Deal makers are more committed to the out-

---

[19]Chuck Palahniuk is the author of *Fight Club* and other books.

come than to the process by which it is achieved.

On the other hand, deal killers often exhibit an "I can't" mentality, actively searching for and finding issues and problems, and working with great diligence to create endless hurdles. They thrive on repetitive and often meaningless process dialogue that results in conclusions like, "We really need to have another meeting." The finish line doesn't matter because they have no intention of ever getting close to it. If you love to create and do and complete, deal killers make your life miserable.

The deal maker/deal killer dichotomy is a business reference, but in every part of life these rather stark differences in perspective and attitude show up over and over. This core distinction between doer and blocker (or owner and victim, creator and reactor) can be considered a fundamental human operating choice each of us makes, and those choices continuously and pretty consistently define our attitudes, values, priorities, methods and outcomes.

If ever there was a time to clearly understand the *modus operandi* distinctions between owners and victims, it is today. In simple terms, healthy creation, decision-making and actions are more closely aligned with ownership. Ownership means you are driven by results. If you find yourself consistently spending time and energy on rationalizing and explaining why you won't or can't deliver results, you are not acting as an owner. The closer you can move to a 100% owner mindset, the better decisions you will make. It will help you be clear in both creating a game-changing plan and in staying on course thereafter. And you can shift the energy spent explaining "why not" toward achieving your desired results.

It's A Choice

Today you may find yourself squarely in a victim mode of living and unable to see a way out. If you are currently embracing a victim mentality, this is a *wonderful* time to be alive. There is a virtual cornucopia of choices available for which blame can be assigned for your inaction: genetic deficiency, poor parenting, oppressive siblings, bad teachers, a myriad of economic and environmental issues, being tired or stressed or both, and so on (and on.)

But another option you have is to take a moment to see *this day* as the one you have been waiting for to begin a shift in the direction of owning your outcomes. Your creativity can be put to work developing a plan for a future that you can own—and then follow with energetic action in the direction of its achievement. Striving to be the owner of your *creative mind* could be the most important commitment you make for survival and comfort in the years ahead.

* * *

A plan created with an ownership mentality is a plan destined for success. It is a plan built with your personal brand of creativity (always best for you) and a bias for action. This might be all the reason you need to exchange the uniform (and results) of victim for that of owner. This act would be a major service to your happiness and well-being as you move forward in life.

* * *

If you are in a room with a number of people and ask, "How many of you are owners and creators?" virtually every hand will go up. When you ask, "How many of you consider yourselves victims or reactors?" it is unlikely you will see any hands raised (because those timid souls have already left the room). If you listen closely, you will likely hear them in the hallway saying things like, "How can they ask that question? It's so demeaning, and it's none of their business! Anyway, I'm sure they are not talking about me—are they?"

Asking people to declare themselves as owners or victims is not the surest way of differentiating one from the other. In most cases you won't have to ask; you can simply listen and hear everything you need to know. It is all there in how they speak about themselves and the world, allowing you to discover their attitudes and perspectives by merely listening. We make our identities evident by empowering (even supercharging) certain words. The words we choose will almost always provide clues as to our status as owners or victims. It is a way to reveal our true colors without openly labeling ourselves. (Even if one is a victim by definition, wouldn't an open declaration of that state of being require a momentary pose as an owner? "I own the fact that I am a victim!")

Owners are conscious, aware and on purpose. Owners

use first-person words, and words of possession, action and clarity such as: me, mine, I, do, can, will, no problem, and so on. These are words signifying ownership and direct accountability. These are the words of a person who takes responsibility for thoughts, actions and outcomes. These are the warrior words of commitment to the battle and of playing to win.

There is power in the optimism of owners—you can hear and feel it. For an owner, failure, rejection, being wrong or feeling uncomfortable are all outcomes that are acceptable, even good. For them, feedback is considered a welcome source of learning and getting better. Owners push, pull, tug or tow themselves out of their comfort zones and take risks— sometimes just small ones to start. But one "risk-step" is almost always sufficient to get them into action.

Victims use words of deflection, deferral, blame and ambiguity, such as: should, they, them, try, not, whatever, can't, might, difficult, impossible, never, maybe, and so on. These are words signifying apathy, conditional effort and anticipatory defeat; the only commitment they make is to transfer accountability (aka blame) almost anywhere other than onto "me." These are weak words typically more closely related to pessimism, procrastination, wishing, hoping and inaction. Used over and over, these words embody, confirm and reconfirm an attitude of avoidance and an expectation of negative results. These are the words of a person who cannot see a way to decide or act, possibly one who is paralyzed by fear.

You will often hear, "I just want to get through my

_____." Fill in the blank with almost anything: day, week, weekend, meeting, wedding, graduation, vacation, life, even death ("I hope I will be able to *get through it* okay."). Victims suck the oxygen out of the room; they can leave owners gasping for air.

A victim can certainly create a plan, but it will be doomed to failure before the ink is dry. Success is generally not in the cards because sabotage in all of its forms is a victim's stock-in-trade. Victimhood reaffirms itself and over time it becomes increasingly difficult to reboot one's preference to ownership.

Usage of some of the words above, in and of themselves, does not render one a victim or an owner. They have to be said and heard in a context that permits the attitude of the speaker to shine through. Consider the following dialogue:

> "I have started working on a plan to get our finances back on track and guide us in the creation of a concrete plan for our future. I would love to have you work on it with me. In any event, could I just get your opinion on something now?"

>> "I already told you I had a really difficult day at work, and I'm pretty tired. Would you just ask one of the kids?"

> "It has to do with the creation of the life plan I told you about. It'll make us less reliant on oth-

ers, so I can't ask the kids to help at this stage. I know you'll enjoy working on it with me once we get started"

"I just don't want to think about it right now. Anyway, why do you always interrupt me right in the middle of *my show*? You're deliberately going out of your way to disturb me while I'm trying to relax! You have no idea how hard it was to just get through work without exploding today. What was it you wanted again?"

"Never mind. I'll just get started on my own and we can review it later."

"Great. Now you tell me, after you give me a headache. Why do you always do this to me?"

It isn't difficult to identify the owner and the victim.

The victim approach represents the antithesis of assuming command of your life and decisions. It suggests a readiness—sometimes even a *desire*—to permit other people to make choices you should be making, so that you can then complain about them. A victim energetically works to create a foundation for placing blame for virtually everything in his or her life on another person, a conspiracy, the weather, their mattress or something else. This creates a downward spiral in life and relationships until it is arrested.

Reinvention from victim to owner requires a conscious rejection of the unconscious thoughts and behaviors that have created "what is"—our current situation. Simultaneously, we must seize our power to purposefully construct the rest of our lives, something we must do based on what's ahead, not behind, and on what we can create, not on what may be handed to us by default.

One more note of relevance. Research conducted by Howard Friedman (best known for his pioneering work on Type A personalities and cardiac problems) and Margaret Kern indicated that higher levels of *conscientiousness* are associated with living longer. Conscientious individuals are less likely to die than others in the same age range. This work by Friedman and Kern described conscientiousness as a composite of responsibility, self-control, achievement and order.

In *The Time Paradox*, authors Philip Zimbardo and John Boyd articulate that future-oriented people are more likely than all others to engage in positive health behaviors, and more likely to *not engage* in health-threatening behaviors.[20] They conclude that negative health-related behavior patterns set the stage for an individual to die sooner. If you need additional motivation to drive your shift toward being a consistent and conscientious *owner*, how about the opportunity to live longer?

---

[20]Zimbardo, Philip and Boyd, John. 2009. *The Time Paradox*. New York: Free Press.

Who Am I?

Most of us cannot help repeating our thought and action patterns. We stay in a sort of convenient trance of "this is the way it's supposed to be." Our minds construct a story of who we are by cataloguing and repeating the thoughts that are most persistent in an effort to attribute order and logic to chaotic recollections jumbled by the passage of time. This story becomes our principal identity, whether owner or victim. We identify with the story and accept it as true—often to our detriment.

We work very hard to maintain our perception of equilibrium by hanging onto events, activities and history that we infuse with reality. Over time, our reshaped and reconstructed memories become well-developed lies that have the aura of truth. We have repeated them so often and so well, and in such a compelling fashion, that we assume they couldn't be wrong. But could they?

You're Fired!

A more difficult question is what to do with the victims, takers, reactors—the *non-owners* in your life? Practice tolerance? Learn patience? Spend your valuable time helping them create a shift in the direction of ownership? For those closest to us—those within our inner circle of responsibility—the answer to each of these questions is probably "yes." If they *are* close, we probably believe in them (or at least want to) and appreciate their value as human beings (or we are related to them and don't have much of a choice).

But what about those who do not fit into one of these categories?

We all have limitations that require the judicious development and enforcement of boundaries. Boundaries are required for self-protection against overload and frustration, among many other reasons. Limiting the access of non-owners to your life and your time is an absolute necessity.

None of us has enough excess energy to pour into the perpetually empty tanks of those whose preference it is to stay stuck. If you do it, you risk jeopardizing your own future by expending your limited energy in the service of victims. This energy can be better used for creating the life you want in the face of much more challenging circumstances than those that existed a few years ago.

Non-owners are net negatives at a time when we need all of the positives we can muster. As you consider the elements of value for proactively creating your life ahead, please think about who you can afford to have in it, outside of those in your inner circle. Victims, reactors and takers all need an opposing force in their lives to feed their habits. You can fill that role if you choose. But, if you stop feeding them with your energy and attention, they will either stop the behavior or find another host. Either way, you will win.

* * *

As a part of your creative game-changing, consider firing those people in your life who are sucking your time and energy without redemption.

* * *

Your willingness to confront this issue will be another indication that you are the proud "owner" of your future, and that you value every minute of your time. When you do this, you will be amazed at the energy shift that will occur almost immediately. There is no substitute for living as an owner. And, you may even live better and longer as a consequence. Ownership and game-changing action are a powerful combination.

Chapter 14

The Self-Reliance Imperative

The question isn't, 'Who is going to let me?'
It's, 'Who is going to stop me?
Ayn Rand

As a woman or man of forty-five today you have a good chance of celebrating your eighty-fifth birthday forty years from now. It may come as a bit of a surprise, but when you turn eighty-five you will *not* be part of a small, elite group of health conscious octogenarians. In the year 2050 you will be but a single voice in a chorus of almost twenty million Americans who will then be eighty-five and older.

If you are twenty-five today, in 2050 you will take your place among almost *ninety million* Americans over the age of sixty-five. This is a demographic game-changer that is not anywhere near its zenith.

Even if there was a sincere desire to act as one, our government will not represent a reliable stopgap support system for most Americans in the years ahead. The fact is that the political system has become so deeply complex and is in such a state of chronic malaise and constipation that the best our politicians can do is arrive at largely destructive and nonsensical agreements that merely keep governmental offices "open for business."

In the private sector, clever financial professionals have worked the holes in the system to create massive cash flow and profits that completely undermine the foundation of our economy. Millions of American citizens have suffered the loss of homes, savings, jobs and self-esteem. In effect they have had their pockets picked. Bernie Madoff was but "Exhibit A" of many unidentified, unabashed profiteers producing nothing of value except huge amounts of compensation for themselves. They were in essence levying a hidden tax on the rest of us. We just didn't know we were paying it until it was too late to object or rise up against it.

Massive reengineering will be required to make our financial institutions, economy, and government not only effective and efficient, but vibrant once again. This certainly doesn't mean that America will not survive, as it most assuredly will. But the complexity and time required for such restoration means that most early generation boomers will not be around to see the results. It will likely take decades to bring about a sustained recovery, and the work to develop one has not yet begun in earnest.

The Power in Self-Reliance

The value of most great ideas ebbs and flows depending in part on their relevance to current circumstances. One of the most insightful and perpetually relevant writings I have come across is an essay by Ralph Waldo Emerson.

Written in 1841 and entitled "Self-Reliance", it is more than anything else an exhortation for individuals to trust and be true to their independence and uniqueness. It argues persuasively against the subjugation of individuality to conventional societal wisdom. Put simply, a perfect phrase for an Emerson T-shirt would be, "I Trust Me."

We have in many ways become a nation of conformists who almost without thinking embrace passivity as the natural state of affairs. Conformity might be necessary in societies where compliance is revered (or required) and independence discouraged. But acceptance of the common is anathema to the American spirit of self-reliance—the reprise of which is now required to catapult boomers and others into a vibrant home stretch for the rest of their lives. In my view, the only rational plan for securing our futures starts at the level of the individual, the only place where self-reliance begins and ends.

We have access to a deep history that testifies to the ability of Americans to think and act independently, to do what is required when the going gets tough. Although many people prefer to believe that hope, in general, and the benevolence of our government will solve the key economic challenges of aging, there can be no certainty of outcome in such reliance. The creation of certainty begins when we trust our individual initiative to get us through.

By 2030, meeting our basic personal needs and maintaining a reasonable comfort level at age sixty-five or eighty-five will have more to do with self-reliance than with anything else. In fact, common sense and self-preservation suggest that we cannot trust anyone outside of ourselves to ensure that these needs will be met. We have no choice but to turn inward for the answers.

It is a very personal game of *self-reliance* that we must play and win. You must make realistic, fact-based decisions with an absolute commitment to self-interest and independence. You have to plan to take care of your basic needs—including paying for at least a portion of continuously rising health care costs or insurance—out of your own pocket.

It is impossible to create your own answer for economic security for the rest of your life without creating some consciously selected, focused commitments relevant to your individual requirements and desires. (See Chapter 17, *Creating a New Story.*) But even if you are certain that you have the economic issues handled, now is the time to consider your plans for what are potentially the most productive and rewarding years of your life.

What will you choose for yourself to ensure that you will live a rich, fulfilling life? You may be at the top of your game after a lifetime of blood, sweat and tears. Is there any reason that your growth and achievements should not in fact *accelerate* as you enter middle-age, or late middle-age, or early older-age—or wherever you are on your life's journey?

It feels a little weird to be exhorting Americans to actively look to the *self* for answers to seriously complex economic and social issues. You might think the line for that ticket window would already be wrapped around the building. If we do not believe in our ability to solve these issues as a collective in a time frame that can be of benefit to us as individuals, what then is the realistic alternative?

It took a long time for most Americans to recognize that many U.S. social and economic markers were on consistent downslides. There was nothing *instant* about the creation of today's circumstances. Do you really believe there is a quick and easy solution for turning it around at the institutional and governmental level *and* for having the benefits trickle down to you personally? You already know the answer to that question.

The antithesis of self-reliance is leaving to others decisions you should be making for yourself. If you choose, it is certainly an option to leave your key decisions to your banker, financial planner, retirement expert, mother- or brother-in-law or someone else. I believe this is a bad strategy for those of us with old-age ahead—meaning *all of us*. You have to develop and commit to a plan for changing your game to do what is required for *you* to survive and thrive in the years ahead.

Even if your personal game-changing plan isn't ever perfect, having guideposts provides the opportunity for modification based upon choice and self-interest as conditions change—and they will. Leaving it to other individuals—each of whom carry the "burdens" of their own self-interest, need for financial security, biases, insecurities, addictions and the like—is playing Russian roulette with more than one loaded chamber. You could be lucky, but the odds are scary.

Get the Emerson T-shirt and proudly wear it: "I Trust Me." Understand that thoughtful action in your best interest is the fastest way to create the life you want. Seriously committing to self-reliance may cause you to appear nonconformist for a while, but to quote Emerson, "What I must do is all that concerns me, not what people think . . . Insist on yourself, never imitate . . . Nothing can bring you peace but yourself." Is there anything more powerfully relevant to be said in our current circumstances? Why not try on self-reliance Emerson-style and see how it feels? I promise that you will be surprised at the personal power you discover.

"Get Outta My Way. I Can Do It."

Even if you are among those Americans who have worked and saved and are well-positioned from a financial standpoint, you have an opportunity to create a more activist approach to the rest of your life. In many ways, changing your game will be more about proactively committing to creating more value and energy in your life by serving others.

The good news is that America was built on self-reliance and independence. Consider the degree of self-reliance it took for the first settlers in America to journey to a new land, see what was there and use the creativity and skills they possessed to begin shaping it into a viable economy. We have an opportunity to embrace the values of those American pioneers—individuals who didn't know what was on the other side of the river or the mountain, but who went there anyway. Many of us represent the downstream generations of those who had to display self-reliance in their daily lives *because there was no safety net.* That self-reliance is in our DNA too; we simply have to redevelop our connection to it.

In many ways, as American citizens we have lost our way. This has been hugely expensive for us as individuals and as a country. But we can recover. Most of us will have to learn or re-learn what self-reliance is, what it feels like and how to live it on a daily basis. This is not a bad thing; in fact, the process can be one of the most empowering and transformative of our lives. It makes little difference if the genesis for this recovery revolution is forced upon us by the current state of the economy or through voluntary choice.

Taking action now has to begin at the ultimate grassroots level—that is, at the level of the individual. Anything else is mere hope, and more than likely it is *misplaced* hope. And another thing: Over the next couple of decades, the intensity of desperation among those who won't or can't move to a place of self-reliance and independence could rise dramatically. I am not suggesting a future state of civil unrest or anarchy. It is not predictable.

But if the government cannot issue checks or food stamps or other support for those in need, people ultimately *will do what they must* to address their requirements for food, shelter and basic medical care. So it will also be wise—at the level of the individual—to consider the means for protecting what you have accumulated from the distress that can be brought about by a further period of economic malaise, the continuing decline of the dollar, as well as physical damage or loss. In the case of certain tangible assets, it means being purposeful about protecting them, and hedging your bets through use of insurance, security measures and the like.

I am not suggesting we are at the crossroads of a biological *fight or flight* choice. But we are at a point in history where, for many, flight is not an option. We will fight. That is what we do as humans when we are cornered, and that is our legacy as Americans. If we have trouble finding self-reliance for ourselves, American entrepreneurs will come up with ways to create it, package it, teach it, and form groups to support it. And, we will gladly pay them for it.

Will You Stand By Me?

Self-reliance is based upon the premise that "I have to do it myself". But it is more properly said, "I have to do it myself, but I can't do it alone." Self-reliance necessarily will include the enrollment of selected others in your cause, as well as your own enrollment in the service of people you care about (or with whom you have an important economic relationship). (See Chapter 18, *You're Gonna Have to Serve Somebody.*)

Once you have created the picture of what you want your future to be, it will be clear that you will want and need support. Think of it as the challenge of building your own personal team in support of your terrific purpose: your best interests, comfort and, in the best of all worlds, service to others. In a business, once the goals are determined, the managers take stock of the available resources and assess how they can best be deployed to achieve success. Then they determine what they need but don't have. The gaps represent places where additional resources and trusted collaborators will need to be enrolled. It is the same process you will use at a personal level.

Consider the creation of your own Circle of Trust (or Circle of Reliance) through which you can fill in gaps in your plan to create self-reliant living. As an example, if one day you face a debilitating illness, do you have a family member or trusted friend who will care for you? If not, could you identify someone who has a similar challenge and enter into a mutual agreement to create a solution? Each of you would become part of the fabric of self-reliance for the other.

These kinds of relationships were a part of American culture for many generations. The selection of godparents for children is one example. Another is that small, independent farmers used to help each other bring in crops when there was only a short span of time to get the job done. This helped them each remain independent by being part of a collective Circle of Reliance.

There are two types of human resources you will need to enroll. First are people you already know who can directly support and encourage your efforts. They don't have to possess any special expertise. They simply have to be trustworthy and willing to stand with you in your process of creation. They may also have resources they can bring to the table; but with or without those extras, you will need a trusted inner circle of collaborators in your service.

Begin thinking about the people it makes sense to have in your camp as you move through the process of changing your game. Look first to people who have a direct, vested interest in your future success. Typically, these people will be those closest to you: family, long-term friends, current and former work colleagues and so on. The common element must be that you trust them to honor their commitments and to provide clear feedback on how you are doing.

Next, identify those people with capabilities or assets that you will need in the service of your objectives. These individuals may or may not be in your inner circle, or even close to it. You may not even know who they are today. But be willing to think big in terms of the potential universe of people out there who can help you in the creation of your desired outcomes. At this point, don't be concerned about how to approach them or what to say when you do. You are now creating your Team Me; there is no need to compromise before you have even begun.

When you do ask for help, you will be surprised that many people actually love to bring their personal experience and wherewithal to bear in the service of others. In many cases, it is a pleasure for them to do it, connecting as it likely does with their own desire to *do for others*. They may even have been waiting for someone to invite them to be of service. You offer them an opportunity for validating their abilities and experience by enabling them to share their skills with someone in need.

In a very real sense you have something to offer in exchange for supporting your personal initiative: the gift of allowing them to be of service to you, and thereby the opportunity for them to create value for their own lives. You simply have to develop an approach that gives them the chance to serve you—and by your asking, for you to be of service to them.

This is an example of the process of enrollment, and ultimately it is always mutually beneficial. Regardless of whether you know someone today who can fulfill your requirements, you can ultimately enroll such a person in your cause if you are willing to take a little risk for big gains. If you can master the process of enrollment—and you can— you will be able to achieve your personal and financial objectives.

The New "Old Frontier"

Collectively, we can and must make a rapid, committed return to self-reliance, to the core concept of individuals relying upon themselves to transform their lives. The American value of self-reliance served us so well for so long. In many ways we are again pioneering in unknown territory, now in a complex world that moves at a profoundly more rapid pace than in the past.

The pioneering of today is neither about seeking a placid, "golden years" type of retirement nor about degrees of failure or success. It is about creating both your own safety net for simple, comfortable living, and a foundation for doing what makes for your own definition of a rich life.

This can be accomplished by having a bias for independent thinking, purposeful creation of active personal strategies, and boldly taking self-interested actions. In short, by living in a state of conscious self-reliance. As aging Americans, we cannot leave this task to anyone else, but that's okay. We can handle it. No question about it.

Chapter 15

Now Is Your Present

Living is really pretty simple. Living happens right now;
it doesn't happen back then, and it doesn't happen out there.
Living is not the story of your life.
Living is the process of experiencing right now.
Werner Erhard

A lot of us have the challenge of living so far into the future that we miss many of life's *todays*.

The immense value in *the now* coalesced for me as a result of discovering Eckhart Tolle's book, *The Power of Now*.[21] I listened to the tapes of him reading his book in that interesting accent of his, and heard his mantra—the word "*nooooow*"— said what seemed like 50,000 times over hours of the readings. I still hear it in my head, and it has been years since his voice was piped through my headphones.

Without intending to deify him, I believe that he speaks of the *now* with the wisdom and depth of a modern day spiritual guru. Hearing (and since reading) Tolle in- spired me to attempt my own versions of some of the com-

---

[21]Tolle, Eckhart. 1999. *The Power of Now: A Guide to Spiritual Enlight- enment*. Novato, CA: New World Library. For a summary of the princi- ples addressed by Tolle in *The Power of Now*, see *Stillness Speaks*.

pact golden nuggets of wisdom he has turned into a stock-in-trade. Here are a few I created that made me feel as though I was in his head but speaking with my voice:

Mastery of your present moment inexorably leads to mastery of the path ahead.

Every future destination reached is solely determined by what we do in the now.

And:

Only this moment need be observed as perfect. The appreciation of this moment is the only path to the perfection of another.

Try it. You will be amazed by the creativity and timeless knowledge you will find inside yourself just waiting to be tapped.

"What More is Needed...?"

Also ask yourself the ancient Zen master's question, *"What more is needed in this moment?"* Immediately answer it without thinking. Just ask and respond. What was your answer in that instant?

Ask the question again, this time aloud and without pausing. "What more is needed in this moment?" Were you able to find any deficiency?

I suspect you will find it impossible *in the moment* to find any fault with it. "What more is needed in this moment?" The one and only answer is, "Nothing. This moment is perfect." Imagine the peace we could have if we were to consciously and consistently ask this question when it appears that our current situation is impossibly overwhelming.

Many of us now have unprecedented economic, social and family pressures. There is no doubt that we must manage our *now* as best we can. How can you now leverage your uniqueness in personality, beliefs, experiences, skills, attitude, perceptions, education, ideas and whatever other attributes may apply in your specific situation? Those all existed for you in your past and still do in the now. They can be harnessed today to create your future.

Tolle writes that it is impossible to be in the future until it arrives—even if it is just a moment away. We can *only* exist in the now, which means that our planning and our preparation for what is ahead can only occur to us in the present, in our current state and with our existing thoughts. Make your game-changing choices now. Waiting simply relegates many perfect moments for creation to your past. None of us possesses the power to recover them.

No Loitering

Thomas Watson, Jr., longtime president of IBM, said, "Lying dead in the water and doing nothing is a comfortable alternative because it is without risk, but it is an absolutely fatal way to manage a business." This is equally true for us as individuals.

* * *

If you permit yourself to stay stuck, making no deci-sions and taking no actions to change the status quo, you will keep getting the results you have always gotten. What you are today is a perfect reflection of what you have done and been up until this moment.

* * *

What is so profound in living consciously is that you can literally change your life in a single moment. Reflective thought can immediately lead to proactive choice, followed by energetic action in the service of that choice. (For more on this, read about the powerful path chosen by professional football player Deuce Lutui in Chapter 17, *Creating a New Story*.)

Here is an illustration from my own experience: An opportunity I had too-quickly grasped in a time of uncertain-ty, and then worked diligently to make a success, disap-peared in what seemed like an instant. I reentered a business relationship that had ended badly a number of years before. In my view the root cause of its end was behavior on the part of my business partner that reflected the punch line of the fable "The Scorpion and the Frog": "I couldn't resist stinging you, it's in my nature."[22]

Nonetheless I denied the reality I had previously ex-

---

[22]Wikipedia. The Scorpion and the Frog.
<http://en.wikipedia.org/wiki/The_Scorpion_and_the_Frog>

perienced and went back for another round. It was unsurprising to any objective observer when the punch line was repeated. Instead of creating my own new story, I knowingly returned to be a supporting actor in the story of someone else—someone whose approach and values were inconsistent with mine.

My Mindshift

Through this and other experiences I ultimately realized a strong preference for having my self-interest squarely in first place and making things happen principally by depending upon myself. I was prepared to accept outcomes tied to my self-reliance. This led to taking an inventory of my experience, attributes, personality and interests and then developing options that best leveraged my strengths and accommodated and minimized my weaknesses. The ultimate result was the creation of my consulting services firm, First-Global® Partners LLC (www.FirstGlobalPartners.com).

I then decided to create an action plan that would embody my unique offer of service. As part of the construction of my plan, I carefully selected words, quotations, references, catalogued "what others say about me" and even found photos that were representative of my uniqueness and my ability to serve others. I put these into an online template at first only accessible by me.

This creation allowed me to read, see, touch, and modify (without consequences) what my future could look and feel like if created in a certain way. It wasn't important for me at the time to actually have the plan completed. It was started, and it was an active creation that helped me prioritize and make decisions in the *now*. It gave me the clarity of vision to help drive my value proposition and service, leading to a (hopefully) perfect future.

I worked at the creation of my game-changing plan day and night until I got sick of it. After a break I would return to it, typically with a brand new thought that I *knew* could really make a difference in the development of my new incarnation. I even started writing to myself in support of the work I was doing on my plan. I actually shared some of those thoughts with others in order to begin practicing presenting the new "Story of Me" to the world. As a consequence of this process working so well for me, I began creating an outline for *Life Expectancy*. I was now a sixty-year-old who really understood that *it's never too late to change your game.*

The success of my work as a game-changing businessman, consultant, author and speaker is based on my experience assessing difficult, complex, perplexing problems and *knowing* that much more can be accomplished, and more rapidly, than most people would expect or believe. Furthermore, during the assessment process key issues can be prioritized and corrective actions commenced *immediately*—or shall we say *now.*

* * *

Almost immediate change can be created if one is willing to abandon the notion that the passage of time will somehow enable better decisions.

* * *

Certainly there are times when having more information will enable better decision-making and perhaps reduce the associated risks. But you won't know until you have real world feedback for the actions you initiate. In a world spinning as rapidly as ours now does, rapid decision-making and, when necessary, equally rapid course correction, together form a winning and, I submit, an often preferable strategy.

Leave Sabotage to Others

Once you have made a commitment and moved into action, why should you play the role of "First Naysayer?" Should you desire it, there are boatloads of people who will provide you with doubt, sabotage and criticism—in many cases you won't even have to ask. Critics abound, often masquerading as owners and experts. But remember: none of them has ever walked in your shoes. It is in fact impossibility for another person to understand all of the variables at play in your world at any given moment.

No matter how it may otherwise be characterized,

criticism includes the rendering of a subjective value judgment. It is essential to the act of criticism (no matter how "constructive") that something be found to be wrong or bad with whatever is being criticized. Some of the generally accepted synonyms for criticism include censure, disapproval, reproach, disparagement, condemnation, denigration, blame and denunciation. When you look at the foregoing synonyms altogether, it makes it hard to fathom that the phrase "constructive criticism" can be anything but oxymoronic.

Instead, please accept and value: mentoring, coaching, advice, opinions and feedback. These can be corrective, but also suggestive and opening. They do not require one party to be right and one to be wrong. If you are going to be a game-changer, you must trust in *you* first and foremost. And if you take seriously critics who judge your work and your progress (if not you as a person) it will make it easy for you to rationalize why you shouldn't try, do and succeed.

Success comes when you keep your focus on "what to do" rather than on "what not to do." This well-known quote from President Theodore Roosevelt puts critics in perspective:

> The credit belongs to the man who is actually in the arena; whose face is marred by sweat and blood; who strives valiantly; who errs and comes short again and again because there is no effort without error and shortcoming; who knows the great enthusiasms, the great devotion, spends himself in a worthy cause; who at best knows in the end the triumph of high achievement; and who at worst, if he fails,

at least fails while daring greatly, so that his place shall never be with those cold and timid souls who have never tasted victory or defeat.[23]

I strongly suggest that as a part of your game-changing process you trust your well-considered judgments more than ever before. *Ultimately, there can be no happiness in living for the approval of others.* Invite input and challenge, but be the owner of your decisions and actions and course adjustments. This is self-reliance at its best.

Carpe Momento

When the chips are down and there is a need for the kind of disruptive change that can create an immediate shift, there is absolutely no point in deferring action to another day. In fact, procrastination probably played some part in creating the situation you find yourself in today. Urgency and immediacy are central to my approach as a professional in helping others make very rapid changes, and they contribute to an effective strategy for personal game-changing plans as well. If your priorities and your direction turn out to be wrong, they can always be adjusted. Give yourself permission in advance to make active errors in judgment.

What cannot be abided is staying stuck and making no effort to change what's not working. There is no value what-

---

[23]Excerpted from a speech entitled "Citizenship in a Republic" given by Roosevelt at the Sorbonne in Paris, on April 23, 1910. http://www.leadershipnow.com/tr-citizenship.html

soever in losing ground because of passivity and inaction. It is much more preferable to evaluate, prioritize, and act *now*. Once you are engaged in *action*, the process of energetic creation will pull you through to the next step. When you act you become a part of the process, rather than examining it from the sidelines as though it is a foreign object belonging to someone else. Staying on the margin—neither in nor out—will keep you invisible and powerless to create your future.

Many of us get into the habit of wanting something more and different than we have in the present moment. The truth of all truths is that this moment—and what is contained in it—is all we have. The shifting sand in your hourglass represents a continuous acknowledgment of the incontrovertible gravity of life. Fully living in the moment is all that is required to move effortlessly into a perfect future.

The moment before has already passed. The moment ahead has not yet arrived. *Carpe momento!*

Chapter 16

A First Step *Is* A Shift

And then the day came, when the risk to
remain tight in a bud was more painful
than the risk it took to blossom.
Anaïs Nin

In becoming an agent of change in the service of *you*, the first step is... *taking the first step.*

Taking a single step moves you into a new position, one from which you can see things differently. If you take that one last step at the top of a hill, you suddenly have a view of a new landscape, a new vista and horizon. Without that single step, your current view of the world—including its necessarily limited options and alternatives—remains your reality.

But with that single first step you can shift your position away from where you are and move one step closer to where you want to be. In fact, having read this far, you are *already* not where you were at the beginning of this book. You are in motion. Your move to start and continue reading has already changed your vantage point and quite possibly your thinking about the options available to you.

You cannot change your game from one wherein you accept the *status quo* to one devoted to creating a new life without freeing up energy to move in your chosen direction. To find it you might have to redirect energy you are currently using to keep yourself ensconced in your comfort zone, surrounded by your favorite rationalizations. It takes energy to *resist* change, sometimes far more than it does to make it happen.

If you continue to simply use your energy to protect your current status, by definition it cannot serve your advancement. And you will need all of the energy you can muster for creating and implementing a game-changing plan designed to deal with the vastly changed circumstances in which we collectively find ourselves.

First (and Second) Steps

Simply commit an hour of your time for thinking about your current game and what might better serve your interests. Then, release just enough energy to take a first step. Taking the step means you now have at least a chance to change the results you have been getting into the results you require. No one else can provide you with the energy you need to create that shift, but that's okay. The energy is not outside of you; you already have it inside, and you can *instantly* choose to see what the view is like from the new perch once you take your single step.

What energy has been awakened that allows you to

take a mere *second* step? Some say that the second step is actually more important because you no longer have one foot resting in your comfort zone. Philippe Petit, (celebrated high wire walker) commented on why the second step can be more challenging: "You see, with your first step, you still have one foot anchored and supported by something solid. With the second step, you have to shift your center of gravity so that your entire body is no longer supported by anything solid."

Compared to Petit's, your own task may be a bit simpler since you're likely addressing it with both feet on the ground (and it will probably have less dramatic potential negative consequences). But, just as on a high wire, if your second step turns out to be *wrong*, you will know it based upon the results you get or don't get. You will have the opportunity to make an adjustment. Without the steps, there is nothing to adjust.

Every one of us knows through personal experience or observation of others that first steps can lead to amazing outcomes. Many times we are not even aware of some of our own significant first steps until much later, in the clarity of hindsight. *We all love stories of overnight successes because they represent hope for us that there is a quick fix for everything.* In fact, however, most apparently rapid achievement simply represents the long-term results of a first step taken long ago, followed by many persistent steps thereafter. Here are two such stories...

Kenny K. of Seattle

At age seventeen, my friend Ken Kirkpatrick started his first job as a teller at People's Bank, one of the predecessors of U.S. Bank. He was offered the job without the benefit of his hiring manager, John Laughlin, knowing that Kenny was a bit shy of the minimum age for the job.

When Kenny arrived for his first day on the job, his new manager, Mary, apologized and told him that because the bank's bonding company had a minimum age requirement of eighteen, she could not hire him. Showing some of the grit, boldness and persistence that would serve him well throughout his life, Kenny said, "You're going to have to make an exception in my case and hire me anyway. Mr. Laughlin told me I was hired, and it's clear that he's a man of his word. I need this job so I can pay for college. I don't want for any of us to be disappointed." But she sent him home.

The next day he showed up for work again. Mr. Laughlin found himself between a rock and a hard place. He realized that this young man was precisely the kind of employee he wanted, regardless of his age. Ultimately Mr. Laughlin relented. Kenny officially started work, enrolled in and graduated from the University of Washington, and he has worked for the bank ever since that auspicious day in 1971. In 2002, thirty-one years after he started, he was appointed president of U.S. Bank for the State of Washington—a post he still holds, doing work that he loves. He was also appointed to the board of directors of the Federal Reserve Bank of San Francisco, Seattle branch. He is still married to his bride of thirty-six years, SaSa, and together they have raised two fabulous, high-achieving children.

He took an insistent first step and the rest is written as his history to date. A work of remarkable personal and professional achievement, to be sure, but not exactly a story of overnight success.

One final note: At age fifty-eight, Kenny was forced to wage a fierce battle with an aggressive form of brain cancer. Because of their practiced ability to move swiftly into motion—and to fight with the indomitability of spirit that is the hallmark of their partnership—Ken and SaSa have, for the moment, defeated this insidious disease. It would likely have taken the life of a man who was less able to energetically begin and persist no matter the apparent odds.

Landau Eugene Murphy, Jr.

In the U.S. there is a television show called *America's Got Talent*. Over the course of a season it features talent competitions among individual and group entertainment acts. One ultimate winner receives a million dollars and the opportunity for a headline show in Las Vegas. Landau Eugene Murphy, Jr. took a first step in the direction of his dream by auditioning for this show. When he decided to make his move, Landau was living in the small town of Logan, West Virginia, making a meager living as a car washer for a local automobile dealership. In fact, his status as car washer was actually a long way *forward* from having been homeless when he was nineteen. Auditioning for *America's Got Talent* was clearly a *huge* vision for Landau, but he took that first step.

At the time, he was an amateur singer who sounded eerily like Frank Sinatra. He could belt out Sinatra's greatest hits with a fabulous, understated style. After he qualified for the show, he went through weeks of head-to-head competition with dozens of other entertainment acts. Tens of millions of Americans ultimately voted for Landau Eugene Murphy, Jr. of Logan, West Virginia, as the top act on *America's Got Talent*. He is now one million dollars further away from being homeless. There is little doubt that he will be a Las Vegas headliner for years to come.

He was bold enough to take a step, and was prepared to hear "no." Instead he ultimately heard "yes"–and the rest is entertainment history in the making.

Timing is Everything: First-Mover Advantage

When the field of play has changed in business, those among the first to recognize the change *and* take appropriate action are sometimes said to have *first-mover advantage*. There are tens of millions of aging boomers as well as older and younger Americans competing for a piece of the same pie that is needed for a modestly secure future. On a personal level, as a first-mover you will have access to many more options than what will be available to those who procrastinate.

If you are one of the first-movers among the aging American population to understand the changed environment and do something about your place in it, you will have a significant advantage over those who wait until everyone else figures it out.

In *Population, Evolution and Birth Control*, Garrett Hardin wrote, "It was learned thousands of years ago [that] natural selection favors the forces of psychological denial."[24] This is an elegant way of saying that those who are willing and able to see the world as it is, can move into action and seize advantage based upon that realistic view.

If you feel you cannot take the first step into action, find someone who will walk with you and help you out of the state of inertia. Reaching out to such a person *is itself a first step* of your choosing, based upon your understanding of how to achieve what you desire. Think of such a person as your personal coach for your Team Me. Coaches today are no longer the exclusive province of athletes and actors and entertainers. There is a coach for everyone. You can choose your own life coach, success coach, executive coach, transition coach (or a coach for anything else)—someone who is exclusively in your corner and who can provide some objectivity, creativity and challenge.

Asking for help in taking that first step toward creation *is* a first step toward creating the rest of your life. It does not represent weakness or procrastination. It represents *your* way and *your* choice. And you are on *your* way.

---

[24]Hardin, Garrett. 1969. *Population, Evolution and Birth Control*. New York: W.H. Freeman & Co Ltd.

Chapter 17

Creating a New Story

Commitment is an act, not a word.
Jean-Paul Sartre

Taitusi "Deuce" Lutui is a Tongan by birth and a gentle warrior in spirit. A long journey from that South Pacific island nation led him to stardom as an All-America football player at the University of Southern California.

However, as a professional football player with the Arizona Cardinals, he settled into what most people viewed as a malaise of mediocrity. When he arrived at NFL training camp in 2010, he brought with him an attitude that was way too casual to be productive for himself or his teammates. His coaches were critical of Lutui's weight—which had ballooned to nearly 400 pounds—and of his neglect of the off-season workouts that would have enabled him to start training camp at an appropriate fitness level.

By NFL standards, Deuce had a small, short-term contract; now he was in the midst of proving why that was entirely appropriate. At the time he even joked publicly that he was the Lindsay Lohan of the Arizona Cardinals because of all the bad publicity he was getting. But the joking was a cover for something deeper. Despite his size, talent and the opportunity afforded him, he was not performing to his full potential, and he knew it.

Change. Now!

Deuce Lutui's fortunes changed in a single transformative moment. Through an improbable connection, Deuce met his off-the-field master coach Steve Hardison between training camp and the start of the regular season. In his first coaching session with Steve, Deuce discovered something that enabled him to instantly trade the story he had been telling himself about being average for one that enabled him to immediately tap into his unrealized potential.

With Steve's help, Deuce was able to see the personal power already present within himself, the power ready to be put to work in his own service (and, of course, in the service of his employer, the Arizona Cardinals). He declared to Steve—and more importantly, to himself—that at that moment he was The Best Offensive Lineman in the NFL (TBOLITNFL) and he would continue to *be* TBOLITNFL from then on. In that single moment of personal truth, he activated a mindshift that would move him rapidly from the lower middle to a place near the top of the heap of offensive linemen in the NFL.

He made his commitment public and the TBOLITNFL movement was born. Due to a convoluted connection I have with George Tupou V, the King of Tonga, I met Deuce at about this time and attended the Arizona Cardinals season opening game with Deuce's life coach, Steve Hardison. In support of Deuce and his commitment, Steve carried a huge TBOLITNFL banner all around the Cardinals' stadium. Deuce could see it from the field and was instantly reminded of his commitment. The banner was also being shown via TV cameras for a nationwide audience to see and wonder about the meaning of the letters. As the NFL mid-season approached, Deuce's reality became one of reaching deep to access a personal commitment and strength he hadn't known was so readily available. He lived it on every down he played during that season.

With his vastly improved performance during the 2010 season behind him, Deuce made the decision to move from the Cardinals to the Cincinnati Bengals. For his transformational improvements in 2010 he was rewarded with the opportunity for a new two-year, eight million dollar contract, starting with the 2011 season. His new deal included five million dollars for the 2011–2012 season alone. He had made this happen in less than a year, and it wasn't about the Cardinals or the other NFL offensive linemen in the league. It was solely about Deuce and his commitment to being the best he could be.

By all indications, Deuce had changed his life and his future in a single powerful moment. He saw and declared his potential. He made a personal commitment to access the part of him that he believed was *already* the best offensive lineman in the NFL. He was then able to harness his immense physical talent and athletic skill and match it with the kind of mindset and commitment that would enable him to utilize it to his fullest. It didn't take years of therapy, or the unpleasant reality of the nomadic life of a journeyman NFL player, enduring trade after trade after trade until nobody calls. He took control of his life and seized the opportunity to make it different. He began living on and off the field as the person he declared himself to be. Everything changed in a single moment with his recognition of the opportunity before him and his commitment to make the most of his unique gifts.

Round Trip

Deuce's trade from the Cardinals to the Bengals (and his lucrative new contract) was conditioned upon him passing the Bengals' physical exam. Among other things, the exam included stepping on a scale to check his weight. In another single, powerful moment, Deuce's world changed again. The scale declared he was carrying 381 pounds; he should have been thirty or forty pounds lighter. The Bengals said, "No, thank you Deuce," and less than twenty-four hours after he left for the promised land of his new contract and team, Deuce was on a plane back to Phoenix.

The next day he signed a modest, one-year contract with the Cardinals, which was accompanied by an admonition from the Cardinals' coaching staff that he needed to immediately and seriously focus on getting some weight off. Deuce's lapse in his TBOLITNFL commitment cost him millions of dollars. Some estimated that he left more than six million dollars over two years on the Bengals' table. If this was the case, it represented about $200,000 per excess pound he carried onto that scale in the Bengals locker room. In football terms his descent was complete when, throughout the next season, still overweight, he was relegated to a back-up position on the Cardinals' team. For the first time in his career he found himself watching from the sidelines as a back-up to someone else—after seventy-two games as the starting right guard at the highest level of professional competition.

"I'm Pretty Sure I'm Committed."

The word "commitment" is overused, and the importance of the concept has become somewhat diluted. But if you care about changing your game for good, there can be nothing casual or part time about your approach.

* * *

Significant change requires clarity of thinking, a realistic inventory of your personal resources, and the ability to engage in purposeful choices and actions.

* * *

Equally important is our willingness to make a consistent, daily commitment to action in pursuit of our goals. Deuce discovered this (and paid a hefty price) by virtue of the natural consequences that flowed from not living a daily commitment to his off-season fitness.

Of course, any of us might profess a commitment that declines in vigor as time goes by, morphing into something we examine from afar, talk about or pursue from time-to-time. If this is our choice when we awaken—for too many days—then we are no longer dealing with a commitment. It descends to the level of something in which you may have *some interest*, but which you no longer consider a priority. Somewhere along the way it ceases to have the consistent urgency that is the true hallmark of commitment. It has instead become a *choice*, something one *might* or *might not* do. It has lost the personal power embedded in a true commitment. Commitment requires consistent, daily, active creation to give it continuing life.

Another way to think about the difference between commitment and choice is in terms of a crisis. In a crisis (real or purposefully created) a commitment will drive prioritization, energy, insistence and decision-making with the urgency that is required. If you can characterize your commitments to yourself and others as solutions to an ongoing crisis, you will have infused them with the energy needed to drive action every day.

Another factor that exists in a crisis is an extraordinary willingness and ability to be creative and innovative in order to get under, over, around or straight through any obstacles. This is true for deep commitments as well. When you are truly committed to solving a problem, ideas percolate and coalesce and simply appear as though out of nowhere. A vision may reveal itself that points the way toward doing a lot more with a lot less. You rapidly sort revised information and circumstances, new variables and considerations, applying what you learn to adjust the direction of your energy and the shape of your commitment.

* * *

Using the forces of constraint and limitation enables doing what is required with greater urgency and less wasted motion.

"Why Are We Doing This?"

Commitments, once made, must be continuously challenged. This is part of accessing the objectivity (the "truth") required to navigate dynamic environments. During many business planning sessions that I led or participated in as a CEO, president or board member, I often asked the following question: "Tell me again, why we are doing this?" The usual response was, "I thought we already decided why we were doing it." My answer: "We did, but can you explain it to me again?"

I knew that when the decision was initially made it was supported by facts and information current at that time, and based on then-available resources, economic conditions and so on. But I also considered it imperative to confirm that the reasons for the initial decision were still valid in the light of updated information. If they weren't, what course adjustments would better help us attain the desired results?

Once you have made a commitment in any area of your life, ask yourself often: "Does this commitment serve my interest in the way that it did when I originally made it? Have I learned or accomplished things that make it necessary to adjust or even abandon this commitment in favor of something else?" I see these questions and the processes associated with answering them as vital, both for mental health as an individual and as part of good market awareness and decision-making for a company.

In a world that is moving so fast, the rationale upon which we based earlier decisions could easily have evaporated. In re-evaluating our commitments we have the opportunity to incorporate new data, different points of view, and new insights based on the feedback and other information received since our initial decisions were made. Don't be afraid to ask these questions. Is what you are doing today still served by the decisions you made last week, or last year, or when you were twenty? I rest my case.

Every Day is a New Day

Deuce's story is one of real and significant transformation. Deuce *did* create a new story in almost every way, and very quickly. He *did* place himself in a position to be among the highest paid offensive linemen in the NFL. He *did* create a new opportunity with a new team that valued him more highly than did the Cardinals. He did *all* of that. But, he forgot something. *Once made, a commitment is not permanent—it is only as good as its daily renewal.*

Any commitment, no matter how vigorously initiated, remains a choice to be served or ignored. In fact, we can and should view this process of renewal as the kind of creative activity that allows us to shape, improve, modify and live our commitments each day. It permits us to pursue the most important interests in our lives and never be bored with the process or overwhelmed by what needs to be done over the months and years ahead.

In another context, this might be the mantra of "One Day at a Time." To energize any commitment, all we need do upon awakening each day is choose how we will express our commitment that day.

Psychiatrist Thomas Szasz said, "People often say that this or that person has not yet found himself. But the self is not something one finds, it is something one creates." We create the best of ourselves through our purposeful commitments continuously cultivated, refined and reaffirmed.

Resistance to (Even) Desired Change

No matter the level of our commitments to change, transform and energetically access our personal power, hurdles and challenges inevitably arise. It wouldn't be life if they didn't. Despite Deuce Lutui's ability to rapidly commit to a new direction, and his ensuing intensive action, substantive transformation happens over time. It is almost never quick and painless.

There is real wisdom in this excerpt from George

Leonard's *Mastery: The Keys to Success and Long-Term Fulfillment*: "Backsliding is a universal experience. Every one of us resists significant change, no matter whether it's for the worse or for the better . . . it doesn't necessarily mean you're sick or crazy or lazy or that you've made a bad decision in embarking on the journey of mastery. In fact, you might take these signals as an indication that your life is definitely changing—just what you've wanted . . . *Be willing to negotiate with your resistance to change.*"[25] (Emphasis added.)

The highest value in the creation of any new Story of You is what you choose to be and do when the going gets tough. In Deuce's case, because of the trip he took from Phoenix to Cincinnati and back he received an even bigger opportunity to change his life again, to become an even more powerful example to the TBOLITNFL Nation that rose up to support him. In fact, his story has the potential to be even more compelling *because of* his weekend trip to Cincinnati and the millions of potential dollars that evaporated with his step onto the scale.

Lao Tzu, Chinese philosopher and author of the *Tao Te Ching*, wrote, "Failure is the foundation of success, and the means by which it is achieved." The good news is that no matter what Deuce does in the future, many others saw what he did to create a shift—one that really changed the trajectory of his life and career—and they have leveraged his experience as a foundation for changing their own lives.

---

[25]Leonard, George. 1992. *Mastery: The Keys to Success and Long-Term Fulfillment*. New York: Penguin Books USA.

Fly a Kite, Sometimes

It may be tempting to distinguish your situation from Deuce Lutui's by saying, "Yes, but Deuce has gifts and opportunities that are exceptional, and he had lots of help. I don't have what he has."

The truth is that each of us has unique talents, skills and creativity that can be tapped at any moment. The clarity and degree of your commitment is the only barrier to achieving what you desire. In terms of support, there is a very likely a network of people in your life ready, willing and able to support a real and visible commitment by you to make your life different. You simply have to be willing to enroll them. (Look ahead to Chapter 19, *Beginning Is Commencing to Get Started*, for an introduction to the art of enrollment.)

When the chips are down and you are ready for your reality to be different than it is, your life can change in a single moment of choice—coupled with conscious commitment. If your journey feels uphill and against the wind, tap into your uniqueness. Commit to allowing it to serve you. I agree wholeheartedly with Deepak Chopra when he writes, "Beneath the fear of being unique, each of us has a powerful craving for as much uniqueness and specialness as possible."[26]

Only Deuce could stop himself from continuously living his commitment. Is it really any different for you? You

---

[26]Chopra, Deepak. 1991. *Unconditional Life: Discovering the Power to Fulfill Your Dreams*. Bantam Books.

can certainly choose to view this now-permanent economic storm as a reason to run for cover. Or you can build and fly a kite, and engage with the storm as a new adventure. It is truly and simply your choice.

Chapter 18

You're Gonna Have to Serve Somebody

Act as if what you do makes a difference. It does.
William James

Committing to serve others is essential for driving rapid game-changing in your life. My friend Steve Hardison represents the ultimate incarnation of someone choosing service as his platform for living and realizing his dreams. He begins and ends his days with the question, "How can I be of service?" Though each and every step he takes is based upon the creation of something outside himself, he completely understands that service to others *is* service to himself and his family. As a successful life coach, Steve has dedicated himself to helping people embrace the vitality of service, and to discover and leverage their unique resources in the service of others. He describes himself as the ultimate coach for personal, business and relationship transformation, and he delivers.

Create Value Through Service

There may seem to be a conflict in considering service to others *and* self-interest as foundational elements for changing your game. In fact, however, self-interest begins with our ability to *create* from within ourselves but necessarily *deliver* outside of ourselves. If you are going to do the best possible job of serving your self-interest, it is necessary to be as proficient as possible at engaging your uniqueness in the service of others.

The first step in such service is the identification and understanding of your differences and consequent uniqueness. (See the next chapter, *Beginning is Commencing to Get Started* for more on this.) These are the most significant qualities separating us one from the other. Whether you are making a living and taking care of basic comfort or are moving in the direction of self-actualization, the best approach lies in engaging yourself in quality, committed service to others.

Depending on what you are offering, it might be okay to randomly approach others and offer your service. But it will likely be more efficient and satisfying if you first give some thought to identifying the best subjects for your service and how to approach them. Your offer and provisioning of service is not "service" if it is not valued by the recipient. Mutuality of the exchange requires a match of the service with perceived value, even in cases where no money is involved.

When you observe people who are masters of service, you find that once they have identified a need they don't wait to be invited. They jump into immediately and begin delivering the service. Before the recipient can say, "No, thank-you," they are already experiencing it. They may or may not have overtly expressed the need. They might even say, "*Stop*"—but then again they *might not*. They may insist you continue to provide the service and *pay you not to stop*.

These outcomes only exist as possibilities if you are unwilling to take the first step in the direction of making *your difference* available to others. You may possess the best solution in the world, but without serving it up, no one will ever know; your uniqueness will remain your most powerful secret weapon, resting comfortably on the shelf in your home, gathering dust.

There is also real power in the *now* of serving others (the *now* as discussed in Chapter 15, *Now is Your Present*). Telling people what you are capable of doing, or what you might do for them at some point in the future, may not create meaningful conversation or engagement. "One of these days I am going to get around to _____, and I know it will be highly valued." Really? Urgency and insistence have value when directly associated with the delivery of service to others. If you can make a difference by solving a problem or addressing a need *now*, you have reached the land of premium performance. The value in the bargain is typically at its highest when both the server and the served are interested and motivated at the same time.

A Small Step

If you are willing to take a small step in the direction of connecting the dots between your uniqueness and your ability to provide differentiated value, consider this: Presume that as you get older you need or would like to supplement your income by $250 a week (you can fill in a number that is relevant in your financial context).

Once you have a good grasp of what makes you unique, think about who might benefit from your skill and where they might be located. Consider how you could make your differentiated service known to them. You could even think about creating a simple web site as a vehicle for telling the story of how your service matches up with their need. (Templates are available online that make this creation an easy process.)

What would it take for you to provide your special kind of service to others and earn $250 per week for it? I suspect that you will answer, "If I put my mind to it, I can easily do that." Think about it in terms of the value you have to provide and how it could manifest in service to others. And just like that, you have just gotten yourself into business as an entrepreneur/elderpreneur. In many locales in the U.S. an extra $1,000 a month can go a long way toward providing a supplement for basic comfort or a hedge for unforeseen events and emergencies.

Remember the differences among self-reliance, self-interest and selfishness. The first two are aligned in the provisioning of valuable service to others. Selfishness, disconnected as it is from a reciprocal relationship with *real service,* is not sustainable over the long haul in a service context. Be first and foremost a committed *value provider* in the service of others. The rest will take care of itself.

Faking It?

In an interview with author Dale Dauten[27], Steve Hardison said, "The question isn't 'What do I want?' It is 'How do I serve?' or 'How do I contribute?' Once an intense commitment to service is where you're coming *from*, you can ask the critical question, 'Who would I need to be to really make a difference?' In other words, you don't work on what you can get, but [on] what you can be and what you can give."

I love the point about being able to *choose who you need to be* to make a difference. It confirms my own experience that we can put on whatever masks and attitudes we want in order to be of service to ourselves and to others. This is a wonderful way of overcoming the fear of taking action. It is a means of overcoming fear that may have us stuck in a place of low self-esteem. It can free us to provide high value service for others.

In adopting a role based on who you want to *become*, you can sidestep such fears in order to take action in your best interest. This can be a powerful step in the process of changing your game. The role you choose to play is still based upon *you*, but it is also informed by your commitment to practicing *who you want to be*. You are simply making the choice to *act as* the person who can deliver the service you feel incapable of doing directly at the moment. And in so doing you are taking another step in the creation of your new

---

[27]Dauten is a long-time syndicated newspaper columnist and the author of *The Laughing Warriors: How to enjoy killing the status quo*, among others.

game. *You have become your own catalyst for change in the direction of your intention.*

* * *

Playing a role by choice isn't faking anything, but is rather a means of accessing different aspects of your own personality, your own capacities; you are still "you," regardless. It is really about choosing a way of doing what is required under the circumstances.

* * *

Consider this dialogue between Steve Hardison and one of his coaching clients about taking action that the client felt would be uncomfortable:

"I don't know if I could do that," said the client.

"So don't be you," Hardison said. "If *you* can't do that, then be *someone else.* Be someone who could do it. Be Brando, be Bruce Lee, be anybody, I don't care, as long as you do it."

Werner Erhard powerfully makes this point about being okay with approaching the whole of life as an actor: "Shift your perspective from living your life to being an actor playing the lead role in a play called your life." My interpretation is, "If as an actor you can achieve what you desire in life, couldn't you be just as pleased with the results as if they were accomplished by your offstage self?" (See Chapter 21, *Meet Mr. and Mrs. Alice Cooper.*) What difference would it really make, and who's to know?

Making It Up?

When I was a kid, my family moved just about every other year. Each time we moved to a new town and I got ready to start school, I thought about how I could reinvent myself, using the opportunity of a new school for a fresh start. Sometimes I wanted to enter the new environment as a great basketball player or a class comedian; other times I wanted to be the quiet type, and sometimes more outgoing. Once I chose to present myself in the new situation as the obvious choice for "class president." Another time I chose "Team Captain."

I was of course the same *me* for all of these roles, but I had the chance to see how each of them felt by being more one or another. I was just experimenting. But, nobody knew whether the *me* I was presenting was the real me or the former me. They didn't have any context but the present and therefore it didn't matter to them. Any limiting dialogue to keep me from being the *new me* was only being heard *in my own head*. In each case, the *me* I chose as the actor in my life's play actually accomplished whatever I envisioned. I brought forth the me that could *do* whatever I was able to *imagine*.

Later I learned that the *real me* is the one I choose as best suited to get done what I really want to get done in my own interests and in the service of others. I also learned that

I could create these results wherever I was and I could start at any moment I chose.

This is the "me" that is inside each of us. This is the "me" that can be unleashed by tens of millions of boomers who are able to view their later years as a canvas upon which to create the life they choose, *no matter what has come before*. Every person has a *creative type* inside ready and able to offer new perspectives and approaches. Being willing to *play the part of a creative artist* opens the way to your unique strengths and differences unlike any other approach.

Attracting Money

Service is also your access point to money. If you serve somebody and do it well, money will flow in your direction. How much and at what velocity depends upon the quality and relative importance of the service you can deliver.

Thousands of authors and speakers—and some charlatans—have implored people to part with their hard-earned cash by offering to share with them how to get and keep money. A cottage industry arose out of the latest commercial reprise of the *law of attraction* concept. People worked at making careers out of single sentences like "Thoughts are things!"—as if merely uttering these words was somehow life-altering.

The law of attraction in its many permutations has been popular as a promising shortcut for people who don't want to serve. But the promise is never real without a connection to serving somebody else. So I can only repeat: if you serve somebody and do it well, money will flow in your direction. It is no accident that Steve Hardison is one of the highest-paid coaches in the world.

Currency, Currents, Circulation— and Attraction

Currency is defined as any form of generally accepted medium of exchange that is in public circulation. The word *currency* brings to mind *currents*: bodies of water or air moving in a specific direction or, in electricity, the flow of an electric charge through a particular medium. The word *circulation* (the continuous motion and flow of something through a system; for example, blood circulation), suggests what is really important in the pursuit of money: movement. Money supply is generally defined as *currency in circulation*, a form of continuous flow through the entire financial system. Procurement of goods or services is a typical way for the flow of existing money to "keep moving through the system."

Money has no real value if it stops circulating. It may provide the holder (or in my theory, the *blocker*) of the money with a psychological benefit of security or power or something else. But, pure and simple, the money has stopped moving—it is stuck in the system and not creating optimal value. More money is created by spending it for goods and services. It is the flow *out* that serves others in the system by keeping the financial system "oxygenated" through active circulation.

So what about the flow of money *toward* you?

What I have described is a closed system. It cannot work without both inflow and outflow. Victor Boc, in his gem of a book, *How to Solve All Your Money Problems Forever: Creating a Positive Flow of Money into Your Life*, concludes that if the force of attraction of money into your life is greater than what he calls the *repellant force* pushing it out of your life, money will flow into you, and vice versa.[28]

Boc suggests that a way to keep the circulation going is to do something he describes as "glad giving." This means keeping money flowing by taking a percentage (your choice) of what you have received from any source and giving it away to benefit others. Tithing (setting aside a part of your earnings—traditionally ten percent—as a gift to a church) is another example of keeping money in motion.

I believe that in order to attract money you have to commit to being a value provider—to service. If you present value to others in such a way that they can understand the benefit to them, you will attract money. By always approaching what you do with a mentality of, "How can I be of service?" you are consistently placing yourself in a position for the flow of money from the person served (or indirectly from somewhere else) to move in your direction.

For a way of putting money into proper perspective, consider the concepts of currents (currency), circulation and

---

[28]Boc, Victor. 1998. *How to Solve All Your Money Problems Forever: Creating a Positive Flow of Money into Your Life.* Perigee Trade.

flow. Money in motion has more real value than money at rest. We could call this, "Going with the flow." There are certainly benefits to keeping some money out of the system in the form of savings or home equity. But money that is *passing through* is money that has a chance to multiply.

In the economic state in which we will be operating for the foreseeable future, the approach of having money multiply has a better chance of serving our requirements than does watching a small amount of money diminish further and further—or disappear entirely—as the value of the dollar declines or institutions fail. Take it to the bank!

Chapter 19

Beginning Is Commencing to Get Started

Relationships are created, they don't happen by accident.
Steve Chandler

The most important thing you can do to change your game is to understand, access and engage your unique capabilities. What makes you different, and how can you access these elements of uniqueness in the service of others? Much has been said and written about the relative value of the various types of coaching available today: success, personal, life and so on. You may have an opinion yourself, but you might have reached your conclusion without any firsthand experience.

I came to a point where I clearly recognized that I wanted to create my future by leveraging my uniqueness. I also knew I could improve my ability to compete for and land more opportunities to provide my unique, high-value service to clients. I was led to an expert coach in transitions, Jim Manton (who, as it happened, had recently written a book appropriately entitled *The Secret of Transitions*.[29])

I worked with Jim intensively for about three months

---

[29]Manton, Jim. 2008. *The Secret of Transitions*. Bandon, OR: Robert Reed Publishers.

to jumpstart my move from my new point A to a new point B as quickly and efficiently as possible. Jim was very helpful to me at a time when I wanted to raise my game to a new level. However, despite this positive shift, at the end of our time working together we both felt there was something missing; I needed something more in my arsenal to supercharge my next ascent. I ultimately identified this as a need to be more comfortable with the *closing the deal* aspect of attracting and engaging clients.

At first I resisted getting into this subject because in some ways I felt that *I shouldn't have to ask.* I thought that given my education, experience and track record it would simply be *self-evident* to every potential client that I have a lot to offer. Not surprisingly, it *wasn't* obvious to my prospective clients, and it was clear that I needed to improve my capabilities in this area.

It didn't have anything to do with *my ability* to provide the service; it had to do with *my ability to earn the opportunity* to provide the service. I had been the CEO of several public companies and a member of the boards of directors of over ten more, but it was evident that despite my extensive experience I hadn't yet mastered the skills required for effective initial client engagement—especially as an entrepreneur without an organization behind me.

It was also clear to me that I had as part of my uniqueness an aptitude for rapidly identifying what is required for a business (and the people in it) to create an immediate shift in the *status quo* and jump into action at the same time. I was confident in my ability to be of high value and service to my clients once we were working together. Partly because of my positive experience with Jim Manton, I concluded it would be smart for me to seek out someone who could help me become skillful with what I then viewed as more art than science—something I soon learned to call *enrollment*.

You Have to Ask to Get

Jim introduced me to my current coach and mentor Steve Chandler. Steve is a coach who has authored some thirty books, including a number of bestsellers.[30] He has led training sessions for over thirty *Fortune 500* companies and is a highly sought after motivational speaker. As it happens, he is also a renowned *master coach* of *success coaches*.

Steve is an expert in enrollment—getting prospective customers, clients, donors, contributors, patrons and others to clearly see that they *must* work with you because of the value of your service to them. It is actually simpler than that (at least to *say*): enrollment is enabling potential clients to clearly see that you can help them. It is a game Steve understands how to play, win and—most importantly for me at the time—teach.

At the time, I did not consider myself a coach. Nor had I been formally trained in sales. As a corporate execu-

---

[30] *Time Warrior, Fearless, 100 Ways to Motivate Yourself* and *The Story of You and How to Create a New One.*

tive, board member and professional advisor I had access to senior sales managers tasked with the real business of selling. I was involved, but more at what I believed was a *higher level* of describing the company, its strategies, unique resources, direction and value proposition.

I didn't consider my work selling. I would simply talk with people about the value our company offered as something in which I thought they should be interested. (At the time I didn't realize that this approach might very well be the definition of selling.) My view was that the work I was doing was different from selling the company's underlying services or products; *that* activity was for *salespeople,* not for me. Color me naïve—and a little arrogant.

After Jim introduced us by email and arranged for the three of us to meet, Steve immediately did something that was critical to my decision to engage with him. *He started working with me before I knew I was working with him, and before there was any reason (real or imagined) for me to resist.* He sent me the following message before I met him in person:

> Dear Jim and Will:
>
> Thank you for arranging for us to meet. In the meantime, Will, I recommend you read my past blogs to get a sense of my unorthodox work here: http://www.imindshift.com/ And if you send me your mailing/shipping address I'll send you some items that will help you understand my work..............and I look forward to being with you both!
>
> Steve Chandler

I already had assignments from him; he was sending me books and materials to start thinking about. How do you *stop working* with someone you haven't even met? Especially someone who opens himself up to you in order to serve you better? What's not to like? In my case, anyway, it was virtually impossible to say no.

We met with Steve in person and he thereafter made a proposal by which I could engage his services. His proposal hit the nail on the head by proving that he had listened to me and then created, in words he knew I would understand (my own language), an offer that would fill the need I had identified. He translated what he heard me say into a value proposition for service by him that was in my best interest. In part, he said, "Our work will focus on the *quality* of the "ask" as much as the *quantity* of the "asks" . . . And, basic to all of this will be our work on any fear, worry or anxiety around 'asking' that currently exists and how we can remove that from your system by practice. We will also re-create your underlying belief system so that it supports asking and makes it enjoyable for you..."

Though I didn't realize it until later, this was my introduction to the process of enrollment—with me on the receiving end as lesson number one.

Enrollment = Enabling Commitments

The best approach to enrollment is almost always the engagement of a potential client or customer in a *dialogue* (preferably a face-to-face conversation) that provides the opportunity for you to *demonstrate* firsthand what it would be like to work together. Steve proved this to me in his enrollment of me as his client, and we have been working together ever since.

Our ability to create together just gets better and better. *I now see that as the essence of coaching: two people co-creating something better, clearer and more actionable than what one can do alone.* The evidence of our work together is in my consistently positive enrollment of the people and companies I know I can help—and want to help—with my unique abilities.

I could not have imagined that I would ultimately see so much value in mastering the art of enrollment that I would engage a renowned expert to help me advance my skills in this area. This was a real lesson in the value of coaching, however it is defined.

* * *

Life is too short to take the time to learn everything by trial and error when there are expert coaches in virtually every area of interest you can conceive of, who are ready to help you.

* * *

By understanding this I took that first, single step in the direction I wanted to go. I realized that if I wanted to be the best I could be at serving others, I needed to enroll them—in our *mutual* cause of being of service to them. And the best way to do this is by *showing them* what I can do for them by beginning to work with them *before* being formally engaged to do so. (This might be characterized as making an investment in *both of our futures*.) What better way could there be for a potential client to make the decision to work with me than experiencing beforehand what it will be like when we are actually working together? (Or more accurately stated at that point: *continuing* to work together, because we have actually already begun?)

If you choose it, a commitment to mastery of enrollment will provide something else of value in your life: you will always be able to make a living. Enrollment is a highly valued skill essential at some level for virtually every organization. It doesn't matter whether the business is public or private, for-profit or not-for-profit, small or large. It doesn't matter whether the offering is a product or a service or both. It often doesn't even matter where the business is located.

The enrollment process can be done in person, over the phone, by video conferencing, by email or by any combination of these and other means. You can be any age and in any physical condition. When the need exists for productive work and a steady stream of income, moving toward mastering the art of enrollment provides you with a way to accomplish this. This skill has value today and always will. (Also see Chapter 14, *The Self-Reliance Imperative*.)

Whether your economic needs are small or great, there

will always be a huge need for people who have the ability to engage in conversation to identify a potential client's requirements and the means of fulfilling them. If you can do this, it means that you have the ability to deliver results.

Leverage Your Differences

Stand up in front of an audience of 1,000 people and say, "Conformity is overrated." You will see 1,000 heads nodding in agreement: "Indeed, conformity *is* overrated." Go to any high school in America and randomly select ten girls in the sophomore class. You will observe quite similar hairstyles, clothing, vocabularies and even voice inflections. There was a long period in U.S. culture when tattoos were considered brazen and radical. Nowadays tattoos are so prevalent in many places that having skin that is *not* inked in some fashion is a little unusual. In those subcultures are tattoos a mark of distinction or do they represent conformity?

Conformity certainly is valuable when expressed in the form of compliance with laws and respect for others and their property. These elements are of unequivocal value. But when it comes to changing our game and making a meaningful contribution in life, the differences rather than the similarities are crucial.

As discussed above with reference to enrollment, one of the best ways to engage in conversation leading to the opportunity to get started in anything is by conveying what the experience of working with you will be like. *You* meaning the unique person that you are, bringing your specific offer of an experience that by definition is unlike any other.

Why does it matter? My belief is that the best in each of us is contained in our uniqueness and that we are best defined by our differences, not our similarities. Often this uniqueness is difficult to discover within ourselves because we learn early on that society prefers people who march to any drum but their own; to do otherwise is to risk the embarrassment and exposure that comes from missing a beat. (See Chapter 7, *Feel Free to Remove Your Mask.*) It is more comfortable for many of us to remain in the community *zone of acceptance*, where differences can be masked and potential unwelcome attention and criticism thereby avoided.

In truth, many people who conform to societal norms often spend their time wishing they could do what *those who are breaking the mold* are doing. How often do you meet another human being who has a dream they would like to pursue, but who sticks to the *status quo* for fear of failure or of breaking the mold?

Our most profound legacies will not arise out of our conformity. Our greatest potential for impact rests in our differences, in how they are cultivated, pursued and expressed. If you desire to remain active in the mainstream as an older adult, you can leverage the advantages of education, experience (including what you have cataloged in a well-developed failure resume) and the seasoning and wisdom harvested from years of living.

These differences can be leveraged in your move toward self-reliance, whether that move is driven by economic necessity, a desire to contribute in new and different ways, or simply to be more energetically engaged in living. This is the essence of full engagement in life and enrolling others in order to both serve them and to serve your interests.

Now is the time to think purposefully and discover how to showcase these differences to stand out from the tens of millions of other boomers. In fact, this concept of focusing on our uniqueness is valuable for people of all ages; it is a great way for younger people to unleash their power to create a more secure (and interesting) future for themselves.

How can you harness the power of your uniqueness to earn greater opportunities for the rest of your life? If you need to create income as a free agent, what specific value can you provide that might be considered expert or of above-average value? How can you hone your enrollment skills and convey your uniqueness and value? Making this assessment is a task that must start with you, but along the way you can solicit the help of others to aid in identifying strengths that you might not recognize in yourself. Aren't you curious? Ask family members and trusted friends or colleagues: "What do you see in me that I might call my own—something that not everyone has?" You might learn some illuminating things. You might even get some compliments. And in asking you will be proving your readiness for a shift in your life.

Chapter 20

"Do You Have a Minute?"

*Playing to win is going as far as you can
using all that you've got.*
Larry Wilson

One of the originators of *"The One Minute..."* concept
was Larry Wilson. He wrote a book with Spencer Johnson,
M.D., entitled *The One Minute Salesperson*.[31] To the best of
my knowledge, this was the first time anyone had suggested
that improvements in sales could come about as the result of
focused, very short-term efforts. Released in 1984, the book
sold more than a million copies.

I first met Larry when he was leading the Pecos River
Learning Center, an experiential learning facility near Santa
Fe, New Mexico. It was founded with the objective of gathering leading thinkers and facilitators in the areas of human
motivation, creativity, change management and culture
change. The purpose, as envisioned by him, was to create

---

[31]It was followed by several others authored or co-authored by Larry,
including *Changing the Game: The New Way to Sell*; *Stop Selling, Start
Partnering: The New Thinking About Finding and Keeping Customers*;
and *Play to Win!: Choosing Growth Over Fear in Work and Life* (the
latter with Ken Blanchard and Hersch Wilson). Spencer Johnson thereafter extended the One Minute series with several additional books and
later wrote, with Ken Blanchard, the bestseller, *Who Moved My Cheese?*

unique ways of helping individuals and teams prepare to handle the uncertain future by discovering and then reaching their highest levels of personal potential and performance.

The means was the utilization of challenging outdoor events ("ropes courses") to enable teams of business people, educators, athletes and many others to support one another in conquering situations that were out-of-the-box for most of those in attendance.

At one of the courses I attended, College Football Hall of Fame Coach Lou Holtz[32] and his University of Notre Dame coaching staff were there working on their own teamwork skills—despite the fact that they were already operating at a championship level of performance. This was not an out-of-the-box program for *them,* but was another way of pursuing the fractional advantages in key performance categories that mark the differences between consistent versus occasional success.

To be declared the winner in many competitive situations in life you only have to be slightly—not massively—better than the competition. Thus the emphasis is on being just a bit better than the competition at the key elements of the specific game. For example, in football it might mean blocking for the quarterback so that he has a half a second longer on average to complete a pass. Even one extra completion in a game might directly or indirectly lead to a win versus a loss.

---

[32]Coach Holtz's autobiography is *Wins, Losses, and Lessons.*

The ropes course challenges at Pecos River were coupled with classroom sessions relating the lessons learned outdoors to the day-to-day challenges faced by the participants in their specific work and life situations. By this point in his career, Larry Wilson had honed a complex, multi-faceted learning system into a powerful and highly focused set of principles for personal and team development. In hindsight it seems there was "nothing new under the sun" in the individual elements of his program, but the combination, clarity and delivery made it unique and memorable.

Very Rapid Planning

One of the work sessions was initiated by breaking into small groups to individually identify values, purposes, priorities and life plans in very foreshortened time frames—I mean *minutes*: three or five or eight. Participants shared their conclusions with the smaller group. This was my introduction to the concept of planning by forcing—through the constraint of time—rapid access to what one already knows. This is a painless yet powerful way to shove deferral out of the way. I took several teams from different companies to work with Larry and his group with much success, but I also applied the approaches in my personal life.

His approach of rapid planning as a way to get on the road to success without delay, still strikes me as an incredibly powerful way of taking a first step and getting into motion, into action. In fact, so much so that I have integrated it into every aspect of my life, business and personal.

Many participants were at first intimidated by the brevity of time allocated for articulating their position on, in some cases, really important life issues. For example: "What is your life's purpose? You have seven minutes..." But since it was both an individual and a group exercise, each person could see how others were making it work and any trepidation quickly fell away in the energy of the challenge. You realized it could be done because others were doing it.

Remarkable, and in some cases truly life-changing, outputs were created seemingly out of nowhere in a *matter of minutes*. The fact of the matter is that the raw material is already present inside each person but sometimes needs to be forced out. Creating a very limited time to produce results turns the process into an urgent, focused one.

I have brought the concepts of rapid and focused short-term planning into several of the companies which I have served as CEO, president or a board member. I have also successfully worked with individuals (some who call me "coach") in need of very rapid changes in their thinking and approach to life. In many of these cases, the application of the principles outlined in this book led to the development of successfully implemented plans for change that were at least as effective as those requiring considerably more time and effort.

If I had stayed in touch with Larry Wilson I would have been a willing, grateful student of his for another twenty years. But because I didn't, he ended up as an inspiring figure in my life rather than my personal mentor. By my definition, a mentor knows the purpose for which he or she is being sought out, while a more distant figure of inspiration doesn't necessarily know who they are inspiring—but they can still make a significant impact in people's lives. Larry made such an impact on me.

Is there someone who has been influential in your life that you should take a moment to recognize? Or is there a person you would like to have as a mentor but haven't yet asked? Such people exist, and they are quite possibly waiting for someone to engage their experience and expertise.

As I was writing this book I contacted Larry Wilson— now 82—and let him know how instrumental he was in showing me a better way to approach living, and that I was in the process of paying it forward for the benefit of others. It was a thrill for both of us to recognize the inspiring effect his innovative approach had on my life, my work and— unbeknownst to him until the moment we reconnected—his legacy.

No matter how impossible it may seem at the moment, I assure you that developing plans for changing your own game does not have to be a complex, time-consuming process. The first steps to changing your game can actually be accomplished in a very short period of time with a focused effort—if you learn to address the right questions. In Chapter 25, *The Truth in Game-Changing*, I address some of the key principles for accomplishing this.

Decisiveness is Crucial

The world is simply moving too fast to defer taking action. Success requires rapid assessment and short turnaround decision-making. I am not suggesting "rapid" as a substitute for "thoughtful." I am simply using the self-imposed limitation of short-times-to-decision as a way of pushing yourself into action. This process must often necessarily proceed on the basis of incomplete information.

On the concept of attacking a problem by developing rapid plans, quick decisions and solutions, Thomas Watson, Jr. said, "Solve it. Solve it quickly, solve it right or wrong. If you solve it wrong, it will come back and slap you in the face, and then you can solve it right. Lying dead in the water and doing nothing is a comfortable alternative because it is without risk, but it is an absolutely fatal way to manage a business." To paraphrase a well-known (and also nautically-themed) thought that supports Watson's view, "Ships are safe in the harbor, but ships are built for sailing."

When I first heard this succinct expression by Watson it resonated with me with the same impact as Larry Wilson's method of rapidly accessing the information needed to create a plan in the first place. Watson refines the concept by pointing out that once you have rapidly created your plan you must be prepared to *just as rapidly modify it* if it veers off course, or if a better course is revealed. Watson's observation underscores the fact that if properly approached, significant problems can be addressed in a much shorter time than most people think possible. Even with a company as large and complex as IBM, if an initial decision is wrong there is almost always an opportunity to reassess and solve it differently.

By moving into action, you avoid sacrificing valuable time waiting for the time when you possess what you believe is all of the information necessary for a decision—which will almost always be *never*. The most effective method for moving rapidly ahead with the least risk is to make sure that the time between discovering you are off course and the moment you take corrective action is as short as possible.

The approach I later developed for planning was based upon the belief that making decisions and staying in motion is far preferable to the time-honored *paralysis by analysis* with which many larger businesses have indulged themselves for decades. I am convinced that failing to keep an organization moving forward by making decisions as quickly as possible is a poor use of resources. *Resources not engaged are like muscles at rest.* Reactivity—as opposed to the proactive engagement of the people and resources at hand to create unique solutions *now*—can become a way of life. Motion enables impact. Think of an arrow resting in a quiver as compared to one moving at high velocity toward its target.

* * *

An organization waiting for leadership is stuck in idle. It risks becoming disinterested in its purpose. It is likely to be incapable of sprinting when an opportunity arises that requires it.

* * *

The better option seems obvious—but every day many people and businesses opt for procrastination and avoidance as their default approach. In practice, this approach offers up control of your life and its options to whoever will step up to decide for you. Often this will be someone who simply wants the opportunity at hand more than you do. This is certainly an option, *a* way of living your life. But in my view this approach represents a game that is begging for change.

Many individuals and organizations operate under the mistaken belief that delaying a decision (or, more accurately, procrastinating) is the safest way through a problem because they will ultimately acquire more and better information by waiting. This is the same kind of thinking that prevents most people from ever changing their games.

* * *

Failure to make decisions creates natural conse-quences as surely as purposeful decision-making. The difference is that in the former you are inert and in the latter you are creating.

* * *

In an interview with the Gove-Siebold Group, Larry Wilson observed that the opportunity for success is most often derailed by fear. He said, "It's actually not the *feeling* of fear; it's the *avoidance* of fear. They avoid fear, which is playing the game *not to lose* . . . We lose our power when we stop taking risks . . . We tie ourselves up in imaginary ropes and hold ourselves hostage to our egos. We think we are protecting ourselves in the name of safety, but we simply don't play the game to win it."

The idea that a wrong business decision will come back to "slap you in the face" is equally applicable at the individual level. But we make very few plans that cannot be later improved when we acquire better information—*because* we got moving. The experience gained by following a plan in *any* direction, right or wrong, always yields information about how to do it differently and, eventually, better.

You Already Have Answers

You can create a plan for the rest of your life using the information you already possess. So why wait? You have the ability to *very* rapidly access the necessary data already stored inside yourself. Take an hour or so to create a plan for yourself. Consider it an opportunity to get to those key answers within. Challenge yourself to complete it in sixty minutes. You will be amazed at how much information, how many answers are immediate accessible.

Imagine you can access thoughts that will give you eighty percent of what you need to take the *very next single step* toward creating a game-changing plan in alignment with your best interests. This is the foundation for purpose-fully living the rest of your life at full tilt. I wish I could call this process "The One Minute Plan for Changing Your Game"—in honor of Larry—but I haven't yet found a way to reduce the process quite that far.

Even if you make a flawed or half-baked plan today, this is still better than no plan at all. Of course, you could always rely on the *strategy of avoidance* expressed so well in this likely tongue-in-cheek quote attributed to Sir John Harvey: "The nice thing about not planning is that failure comes as a complete surprise rather than being preceded by a period of worry and depression."

The only real opportunity to get results different from those we have been getting for most of our lives is to change the things we have been doing.

Tribute

Larry Wilson, an original game-changer and mentor to many; co-author of *The One-Minute Salesperson* and *Play to Win: Choosing Growth Over Fear in Work and Life*; founder of Wilson Learning and Pecos River Learning Center: for his leadership, inspiration and humility.

Chapter 21

Meet Mr. and Mrs. Alice Cooper

In a time when nothing is more certain than change, the commitment of two people to one another has become difficult and rare. Yet, by its scarcity, the beauty and value of this exchange have only been enhanced.
Robert Sexton

There are many things you might anticipate upon reading the name "Alice Cooper" in the title of this chapter. I would guess that none of them includes the term "iconic marriage."

There are few corners of the world where the name Alice Cooper is unknown. His history as a pioneering and long influential rocker is well-chronicled. Although now in his sixties, Alice still goes on tour for about six months every year. This aging boomer still rocks the house to sold-out concerts all around the world. In the summer of 2011 alone he performed fourteen concerts *just in Russia*. At the time of this writing his schedule for this year already includes sixteen shows on three continents. If ticket sales are a relevant measure, Alice is more popular than ever, especially in many countries outside the U.S. As he put it in a recent interview: "Everyone's interested in Alice again. I'm having *yet another* second coming."

Alice was a pioneering musical force in the 1970s for many then teen-aged baby boomers, and he still showcases his special brand of rock-and-roll musical theater for their children and grandchildren. A typical audience today includes people born in at least five different decades. He is still sought after today because he remains a vibrant professional musician and master showman—the macabre provocateur who has packed concert venues for generations. Even in his sixties, he has not surrendered his vitality to the memories of his past. He is making new memories in his life and career every day.

Alice was inducted into the Rock and Roll Hall of Fame in 2011. He serves as yet another point of proof that traditional societal perceptions about turning sixty or seventy have been blown to pieces. Like Alice, many aging boomers, through hard work and persistence, have positioned themselves to perform at very high levels for their next several decades of life.

A few years ago my son Austin had the good fortune to work part-time for the Solid Rock Foundation, a non-profit group founded by Alice and his wife Sheryl. Its mission is creating positive outside-of-school alternatives for at-risk teens. I met Alice at that time and also had the good fortune to meet his wife Sheryl. It didn't take long to understand that he is a devoted family man and that his wife is a full partner in life and in the business of Alice, Inc. They have been married for more than thirty-five years and have three children; they have created a lasting marriage that is the envy of everyone who knows them.

I wasn't expecting to be so impressed by their marriage, but it is clear that it has provided Alice with a secure and stable foundation as a creative artist in a dynamic business. His type of work is of course well known for its many temptations. But the Cooper marriage proves that a loving home and family can be a big part of success regardless of work environment and distractions.

The Angel

In an interview he gave to Lonn Friend of www.KNAC.com, Alice admits that during the early part of his career he "was a totally functional alcoholic, probably the most functional alcoholic ever. I never missed a show. I never stumbled. I never slurred a word."[33] In the mid-1980s he simply stopped drinking, and he has abstained ever since. He attributes his success in this area to divine intervention and the arrival (and persistence) of an angel—Sheryl Goddard.

Sheryl had started dancing at age six, taking ballet lessons, and as a teen she danced and portrayed characters at Disneyland. She and Alice met while Sheryl was a dancer on Alice's epic "Welcome to My Nightmare" tour during the 1970s. They were married in Mexico in 1976. In their early years together she appeared on stage with Alice many times,

---

[33]Friend, Lonn. 2001. Alice Cooper: Prince Of Darkness/Lord Of Light. <http://www.alicecooperechive.com/articles/index.php?showmag=knac &showart=011019>

most often as "Ethyl" for showcasing one of his signature anthems, "Only Women Bleed". She has continued to dance for most of her life since that time, and she has studied with some of the dance community's top names, including Ruth Page, Robert Joffrey, Joe Tremaine, Glen Tetley and Michael Kidd. She owned and operated a dance studio for a good part of her adult life and has earned awards for her choreography.

Sheryl and Alice have a very stable home life, and it has nothing to do with the adulation heaped on the on-stage Alice. No matter what demands and opportunities arise because of his career, their family takes precedence as one of the most important commitments in their lives. For all of the seemingly radical on-stage antics, Sheryl and Alice are completely down-to-earth believers in traditional values. For them, this includes a strong and loving relationship as marriage partners for over thirty-five years, a supportive and warm home environment for their kids, and deep and unapologetic religious beliefs. You can feel these values when you are in their presence.

"It's An Act. I Mean It."

Since conquering his addiction to alcohol, Alice continues to counsel other rock musicians battling addiction problems. He told Billboard.com, "I've made myself very available to friends of mine—they're people who would call me late at night and say, 'Between you and me, I've got a problem.'"[34] In 2008 he received the Stevie Ray Vaughn Award for his efforts in helping recovering addicts. Regarding this, he said, "I think the older bands are a lot hipper than the younger bands when it comes to the drinking and drug thing, because we've been through it." He cited musicians like Slash and Ozzy Osbourne. "All you need is for one guy to drop dead next to you until you get a real clear picture of it... I don't think you need to die for your art."

Alice believes that spiritual awakening is happening around the world. "It's obvious humanity is craving answers directly born of awareness," he said in an interview posted at www.jesusjournal.com. "That's the healthiest thing I've seen in a long time because there is something better and everybody's gotta find it in their own way. People aren't feeling fulfilled by how many cars they own or the size of their stock portfolio. Even the addicts are saying, 'It doesn't matter how many drugs I take, I'm not fulfilled. This isn't satisfying.' There's a spiritual hunger going on. Everybody feels it. If you don't feel it now, you will. Trust me. You will." [35] This is the thoughtful, spiritual Alice talking—offstage.

In a KNAC.com interview with Jeff Kerby, Alice spoke of how he separates himself from his onstage character, and why this is so important for his life:

---

[34] 2008. Alice Cooper Receives MusiCares MAP Fund Award. Billboard.com. <http://www.billboard.com/news/alice-cooper-receives-musicares-map-fund-1003791560.story#/news/alice-cooper-receives-musicares-map-fund-1003791560.story>
[35] 2006. Alice Cooper is a Christian. JesusJournal.com, March 28. <http://www.jesusjournal.com/content/view/79/85/>

You have to remember though who my older brothers and sisters were—guys like Jim Morrison and Keith Moon and all the people who were living that life. After they all died, I just sat there and went, "...if one generation is going to learn from the next, the truth is going to have to be that you don't have to die to be your character." I figured then that I had better be able to separate the two. When I go on stage as Alice to this day, I play Alice to the hilt—I play him for everything he is worth, but when I'm offstage, I never think about Alice Cooper. He never occurs to me . . . I walk off stage though and I turn away from the audience, I go back to being me again. Whenever I see an audience, that's when I turn into Alice. If there was no audience there, there would be no reason to be Alice. If I tried to be Alice Cooper all the time—I'd either be in an insane asylum or in jail or dead.[36]

All of us, in a certain sense, are also onstage whenever we leave our homes and enter mainstream society. (See Chapter 18, *You're Gonna Have to Serve Somebody*.) We can be whomever we want and do whatever we need in order to accomplish our goals. This is a true possibility for everyone— it simply requires making a personal, conscious choice.

As we can see in Alice's case, a strong marriage and family can serve as a stable counterbalance to the rigors of our own onstage activity. In the case of the music industry, there are many sad stories of people who could not separate the stage character from what truly matters, and who actually did die for their art.

---

[36]Kerby, Jeff. 2005. Kerby's Exclusive Interview with Metal Icon Alice Cooper.<http://www.knac.com/article.asp?ArticleID=3884>

For those who can view their career requirements as purposefully-selected incarnations without succumbing to the need to stay in character, success can be sustaining. Though it is too early to know if the appeal of her persona can cross generations over decades, Alice identified rock diva Lady Gaga as the female version of him. "She created a character named Lady Gaga and wrote songs for Lady Gaga, just as I write songs for Alice," he said. "But when you meet her offstage, she's nothing like that person . . . and neither am I." If you have seen Lady Gaga interviewed as Stefani Joanne Angelina Germanotta (her given name), it is clear that she is thoughtful, grounded and articulate. So, of course, is "Alice Cooper"—a.k.a. Vincent Damon Furnier.

A Solid Rock

In a challenging, fast-paced world rife with opportunities to go off the path of goodness, the Cooper marriage has thrived. "This is a very difficult time for a lot of American families, bringing with it extra stress on marriages," said Alice. "I believe that staying committed to your partner and your family is the best foundation upon which to build a secure future." He continued, "Our marriage is the most secure thing in our lives. If everything else fails, we've still got each other." As for fidelity, Alice maintains that, "If either of us found the other with somebody else, we'd kill both parties." Sheryl adds, "Our kids have an intact family and the security of two parents who are honestly sick in love with each other."

Sheryl and Alice Cooper have succeeded in building a lasting, loving marriage while traversing a career in an industry known for its "sex and drugs" appeal—not to mention that they have worked together in music and in life across the decades—in itself an amazing accomplishment. There is no doubt that whatever the world throws their way as two among tens of millions of aging boomers, they will find a way to succeed by holding tight to each other and keeping their family close. The tenacity of their relationship has been a great part of their success outside their home, as well as enabling a wonderful life within it.

The solidarity represented by the Coopers' life together is an inspiration for boomers looking for anchor points in the economic and societal disruptions we will encounter during the balance of our lives. The proactive creation and nourishment of such relationships is possible for everyone— whether in the context of traditional marriage or otherwise— and in many ways they provide a rational counterweight to the instability now thrust upon boomers. Such relationships are also great places to return to after *being who you need to be* to make it happen in your world, on your own personal stage.

Chapter 22

Technology: You Can't Win if You Don't Play

We live in a society exquisitely dependent on science and technology, in which hardly anyone knows anything about science and technology.
Carl Sagan[37]

Six out of seven American homes today have broadband internet access and ninety percent of Americans are online to one degree or another. But beyond simply possessing this essential online access, individual boomers must also embrace and master at least some of the most current innovations in personal digital technology if they wish to remain a productive part of society. In this endeavor your current chronological age could not be more irrelevant.

Consider the following statistics, which are averages from a variety of recent data reports:

- 770 billion—Number of Facebook page views per month.

- 850 million—People on Facebook (70% outside the

---

[37]Carl Sagan is the author of *Cosmos, Contact,* and *The Demon-Haunted World: Science as a Candle in the Dark,* among other books.

U.S.) sharing 30 billion pieces of content (links, notes, photos, etc.). Facebook estimates that 50% of users log on every day.

- 28 million—Estimated number of people on Facebook over the age of forty-five (just in the U.S.). Age fifty and older is the fastest growing user age group.

- 150 million—The number of blogs on the Internet (as tracked by BlogPulse).

- 100 trillion—Annual number of email messages sent (about 89% were considered spam, ugh (Pingdom).

- 200 million—Number of tweets per day on Twitter. 7.7 million people are currently following Lady Gaga (@ladygaga).

- 3.5 billion—The number of videos watched per day on YouTube.

- 5.3 billion—The number of mobile wireless subscribers (77 percent of the world population.) India and China collectively added 300 million new mobile subscriptions in just the past year.

This is but a small sampling of the day-to-day impact of applied digital technology. These numbers will increase (and quickly pale) as mainstream technology platforms grow in scale, speed and ubiquity. If you are reading this book ten years after its initial publication, you will probably laugh out loud at how miniscule these data points have become, and maybe even wonder whatever happened to some of the dominant social networks that I referenced.

You Can't Win if You Don't Play

It is simply no longer a possibility for a person of any age to stay on the sidelines of the digital revolution but still remain a part of mainstream living. Who would want to be a mere observer anyway? I have worked in the technology world for most of my career, and I understand it better than most. When it comes to personal digital devices, software and applications, though, I am plenty challenged. But I have made an absolute commitment not to allow my discomfort with new technology get in the way of staying on the cutting edge of personal technology resources. I recommend making this effort even it is a bit intimidating or uncomfortable.

Many existing personal information technology devices clearly make our business and personal lives much more efficient, effective and interesting than they would be otherwise. They are necessary tools for boomers (and virtually everyone else over the age of three) to compete and remain vital in the world today.

If you want to be an effective and informed worker, parent, grandparent, teacher, college student or even volunteer—you cannot simply stand by as waves of new technology wash over you. Stay curious and informed. If you are over forty-five (or even over seventy-five), make it a priority to acquire the latest digital tools and learn how to use them. In doing so, you will be enhancing your relevancy and ability to participate in the mainstream workforce and community. You will also likely improve the quality and quantity of connections and interactions with others who use these technologies, such as your children, grandchildren and perhaps even your parents.

Consider these predictions on the impact of technology on work and workers in the not too distant future (from "The Rise of Generation C," a Booz & Co. paper):

> As 24/7 connectivity, social networking, and increased demands for personal freedom further penetrate the walls of the corporation, corporate life will continue to move away from traditional hierarchical structures. Instead, workers, mixing business and personal matters over the course of the day, will self-organize into agile communities of interest. By 2020, more than half of all employees at large corporations will work in virtual project groups.

> These virtual communities will make it easier for non-Western knowledge workers to join global teams, and to migrate to the developed world. As they do, they will bring with them the innovative ideas and working behavior developed in their home territories. Moreover, the proliferation and increasing sophistication of communication, interaction, and collaboration technologies and tools, and the economics of travel itself, will result in knowledge workers' traveling much less frequently.[38]

---

[38]Friedrich R, Peterson M, Koster A. 2011. The Rise of Generation C. booz&co, February 22, Strategy & Business section. <http://www.strategy-business.com/article/11110?gko=64e54>

This scenario will clearly be advantageous for older workers as well: energy can be conserved for working instead of commuting, and expenses can be reduced by using the home as a base for earning income. Productive work and contributions can be accomplished no matter where one lives.

Questions with Immediate Answers

You can keep your brain vital and sharp by instantly seeking the answer to any question that comes to mind at any hour of the day or night. With the technological innovations now available to all of us, you are continuously mere seconds away from answers. Continuous learning must be an integral commitment for the remainder of your life. Committing to this approach will enable you to remain a vital part of society forever, in work and leisure, family and community, and in all the activities you care about.

Technological tools and their applications represent common ground for discussion among persons of all ages, and informed users will find a steady stream of new opportunities and interests in their lives. The impact on the ability to work "virtually" is enormous. See the next chapter, *Free Agency*, for more on the changing world of work and the opportunities enabled by technology.

But staying current is not simply a matter of "keeping up" or "staying even" with the younger generations. In fact, the forty-plus crowd possesses significant work and life advantages that will enhance their use of the latest technologies. These advantages can include more extensive education, experience, work history, wisdom, better work habits (such as working smarter, with fewer interruptions and distractions) and an intimate hard knocks understanding of the competitive rules and politics of the workplace.

The virtually uninterrupted connections of the Alphabets (Generations X, Y and Z, among others—see Chapter 12, *Musical Chairs*) to social networks and gaming have in many ways pushed them further away from an appreciation of principles such as personal productivity and self-reliance. In this area boomers have an advantage that can be exploited, if it is seized now. Don't let a reluctance to engage with technology be the reason another person of any age takes your place at work or even in a social context—and with it your ability to stay self-sufficient and relevant for more years ahead.

Digital Future

Microsoft and AARP joined forces to sponsor research sessions that allowed baby boomers to share their thoughts and attitudes about technology. The result, "Boomers and Technology: An Extended Conversation," was compiled by Michael Rogers.[39] One of the surprising conclusions was that out of every age group, consumers in their fifties show the

---

[39]Rogers, Michael. 2009. Boomers and Technology: An Extended Conversation. AARP.org.<http://assets.aarp.org/www.aarp.org_/articles/computers/2009_boomers_and_technology_final_report.pdf>

highest likelihood of purchasing consumer electronics. More interesting was what the participants expressed about the kinds of near-future technological applications they would find valuable (the benchmark year used was 2019, fifty-five years after the youngest of the boomers was born).

They were asked to base their answers on technology that was either coming to market in the relatively near future or which seemed feasible over the next decade, along with their own interests. Following are edited summaries of some of the conclusions from the referenced report:

- Health Records. Boomers want to be confident about online security and privacy. When they have that level of comfort they will be early adopters of electronic health records—some even choosing to have them implanted in their bodies as tiny chips. They will also maintain their own medical records online using digital diagnostic devices to upload their vitals and test results.

- Gene Scanners. Boomers will buy low cost gene scans, the outputs from which can be combined with their existing health data. They can participate in personal health social networks and connect with people who have similar genetic makeups and markers to compare histories and notes.

- Large Display Mobile Devices. Boomers will demand mobile phones with built-in projection capability: push a button and the image is projected in very large scale on the wall. Expect to see prescription lenses that are connected wirelessly to mobile devices. The display might appear on the lower half of the lens —in what used to be the bottom (reading) part of bifocals.

- **Boomer Social Networks.** Boomers will be linked in myriad ways with their friends and colleagues and connected with the lives of their children and grandchildren. Personal videoconferencing will be commonplace.

- **Teleconference Mastery.** Boomers who are working full-time or even part-time will become the masters of teleconferencing. They will have the choice of moving to a pleasant and lower cost locale, yet stay in the midst of the action.

- **Secure Identities.** As boomers insist upon better security online, better means of assuring that you are "you" will develop. Identity management is a new science delivering the equivalent of a driver's license or passport—improving security but also forcing better online accountability.

- **Ubiquitous Digital Payments.** The connected mobile multi-purpose device will become both a credit card and cash equivalent, and will extend the forms of digital cash and payments (the electronic wallet) anywhere and anytime, with high security and high confidence.

Rogers summarized: "It's a mistake to view the boomers as a generation whose technology habits will remain fixed going forward. They're nearly as likely (78 percent to 83 percent) as those 18-34 to say they're "comfortable" or "very comfortable" shopping for new technology."

There is a better chance of getting and staying employed or otherwise being productive as an aging American if you can muster a deeper interest in *the world driving the world*: applied digital technology. Whatever your thoughts may be about how to engage with the life ahead of you, please incorporate some enthusiasm for the power, knowledge and efficiency that ubiquitous high-speed connectivity, digital devices and apps can bring into your life.

Remaining informed and up-to-date will convey your currency in the modern world and, more importantly, enable you to utilize these powerful tools in the service of changing your game as you so determine.

Chapter 23

Free Agency

It is no use saying 'We are doing our best.'
You have got to succeed in doing what is necessary.
Winston Churchill

Many people in America are now in business for themselves, and more soon will be—by choice or necessity.

The viability of traditional approaches to work is in question due to the fallout from fragile economic conditions in the U.S. and the ripples of global competition onto our shores. In *Free Agent Nation*, Daniel Pink writes, "We used to have a system in this country where companies offered employees security, and employees offered companies [their] loyalty. That bargain has come undone. Anybody who still believes that is a fool."[40] In fact, the undoing of this bargain has become old news.

I believe the way forward will require a new kind of *free agency*, one that beautifully fits aging boomers and other Americans who have been "assumed" out of the work-force—as in, "We assume (for any number of *good reasons*) that you are not going to be here anymore"—or inspired by the lure of entrepreneurship in almost any form.

---

[40]Pink, Daniel. 2002. *Free Agent Nation*. New York: Warner Books.

We are free to create an offering in the service of others based upon our unique ideas and experiences. In many cases you can now be productive wherever you live—whether that's near a traditional office building, in a house in the woods or on a farm with a high-speed connection and a smartphone.

There are tasks that are in fact best accomplished by stitching together *fractions of work* using a number of skilled people rather than the more traditional approach of single individuals completing entire projects or tasks by themselves (for parts of which they may *not* be particularly skilled). One can make a living by delivering these fractions. To paraphrase an old saying, "If the cake is big enough, you can get full just eating the crumbs."

Carl Camden is the CEO of Kelly Services, a company long associated with provisioning temporary workers (temps) for businesses. The Kelly Services offering has broadened over the years to include the full spectrum of so-called "workforce management." Mr. Camden summarizes the changing face of U.S. employment as one of *movement to a nation of free agents* acting as independent contractors, part-time and temporary employees, consultants and others who flexibly move in and out of the workforce.

He comments, "Jobs aren't permanent, locations aren't permanent, and workers are returning back to a free-agent type of work style. That group of individuals [free agents] in most of the industrialized world is already 25 to 35 percent of the workforce, on its way to becoming 50 percent of the workforce, I think, over the next decade . . . The ability to fractionalize so that [workers] can organize work around their life...is one of the exciting, positive social changes that I see..."[41]

Interestingly, "fractionalizing work" seems to be a modern analog for the productivity attributed to the "...effects of the division of labour," as suggested by Adam Smith in *The Wealth of Nations*[42] (first published in 1776). How could participation in this system work for you? Could it be a key element in changing your game to seize the opportunities beginning to appear for first-mover boomers?

The concept of free agency is a sort of reincarnation of traditional entrepreneurship. Economist William Baumol comments that the entrepreneur is "the bold and imaginative deviator from established business patterns and practices, who constantly seeks the opportunity to introduce new products and new procedures, to invade new markets, and to create new organizational forms."[43]

These new organizational forms include established businesses proactively engaging non-employee contractors who want to and are capable of operating with a minimum of supervision and a maximum of entrepreneurial zeal. Given

---

[41]August, 2011. The US employment challenge: Perspectives from Carl Camden and Michael Spence. McKinsey Quarterly. August 2011. <http://www.mckinseyquarterly.com/home.aspx>
[42]Smith, Adam. 1776. *An Inquiry Into the Nature and Causes of the Wealth of Nations.*
[43]Baumol, William J. 2002. The Free-Market Innovation Machine: Analyzing the Growth Miracle of Capitalism. Princeton, NJ: Princeton University Press.

the access and speed offered by today's technology and communications, there are no barriers to many types of businesses being virtualized in almost every way, thereby utilizing and creating new opportunities for a workforce of specialized, efficient and remotely-located talent of any age.

Doing What is Required

It is never demeaning to do what you have to do to make a living. When I was twelve and going into ninth grade I got my first real job. I spent about three years living on the Navajo Indian reservation in Northern Arizona while living with some non-Native American relatives. I was first hired for the summer in a small café where I was thrilled to have the opportunity to wash dishes, peel potatoes and scrub pots and pans. I didn't realize at the time that it was probably a job nobody else wanted, and certainly not one from which happiness is typically expected to be a by-product.

For me it brought pure happiness to be doing something productive over the summer and making money to boot! Not only was I underage for the workplace, some weeks I would work sixty hours with no paid overtime (it was quite a while ago). I gladly embraced the opportunity for the extra hours because it meant more money in my pocket. This so-called "menial" work was a joy for me to perform, and nobody could convince me otherwise.

I continued the theme the following year when I was thirteen. I applied for a summer job as a Navajo Tribal

Ranger's Aide. I didn't realize it might be relevant that I was neither the minimum age of sixteen nor a member of the Navajo Nation. No one asked until I already had the job. So for that summer I was employed by the Tribe as a Ranger's Aide. I happily earned income cleaning campgrounds and repairing roads in Monument Valley Navajo Tribal Park with my Native American classmates.

Merely engaging in these activities created a shift in my thinking that impacted my approach to work for the rest of my life. This shift in belief could not have occurred if I hadn't pushed myself into action by finding and asking for the jobs in the first place. It did not occur to me that because of my age there would be a barrier to me getting some work. (Maybe because of those beginnings of my work life, now that I am at the other end of the age spectrum it still doesn't occur to me that age would be a barrier to doing whatever I choose.)

Simply being present in a working environment of almost any kind will inevitably lead to more options. In the case of my children, and perhaps with a little parental push, this approach has led to them working as unpaid interns and volunteers. In a number of instances this has led directly to part- or full-time employment. This kind of engagement in mainstream commerce, non-profit organizations or anything else opens up possibilities for finding the path to doing what you might love to do. If you simply show up, your ability to be engaged, productive and valuable can be noticed.

Overqualified?

Have you ever heard or spoken the refrain, "I really tried hard to get a job, but I was told I'm overqualified"? It is estimated that there are over 5,000 U.S. Ph.D.'s working as janitors. Over 18,000 parking lot attendants have college degrees, and so do over 300,000 waiters and waitresses (and over 8,000 of *them* have doctoral or professional degrees), along with over 80,000 bartenders, and so on. Approximately seventeen million Americans with college degrees are doing jobs that the Bureau of Labor Statistics says require less education and skill than would typically result from earning a bachelor's degree.

In order to rise to the level of being overqualified you must *de facto* have *passed* the point of being qualified. So when you interview you must first prove your immediate value for the position—irrespective of whether your qualifications exceed it. But perhaps just as importantly, it is up to you to persuade the hiring manager that you *want* the job. If you can do so, you will have already provided an example of your desire and ability to be helpful.

Many overqualified people are making a living because they have checked their egos at the door. These individuals are now engaged in the workforce and are generating income, and have the opportunity to move up to a job that may better match their "extra" qualifications. For now they can simply color themselves pragmatic. Who cares what perceptions others may have of you for accepting work that is "beneath your station in life"? Giving credence to this kind of "caring" is a chronic, debilitating force in American society.

* * *

We almost always care too much about what others think of the choices we make. If you believe in yourself, ignore the critics and the cynics and the naysayers. What counts is being productively engaged—and, through that first step, creating more options for yourself.

"Will Work for Ideas"

Israeli technology leader and innovator Orna Berry, Ph.D., was quoted by Carl Schramm in *Entrepreneurial Imperative*: "Israel is entrepreneurial because as a political and cultural matter my country is unavoidably insecure. *The discomfort of this insecurity led our nation to a life of innovation, creativity, and economic entrepreneurship as a means of controlling our destiny.*"[44] (Emphasis added.)

Israel's entrepreneurial imperative thus reflects pragmatism in the face of a high level of national insecurity. But beyond the particulars of this situation, the general principles apply equally to entrepreneurship driven by the *economic insecurity* or discomfort of individuals anywhere in the world.

We do what we have to do when it is required. If you are uncomfortable being unemployed—or even at the

---

[44]Schramm, Carl. 2006. *Entrepreneurial Imperative*. New York: HarperBusiness.

thought of it—you have an opportunity to reframe your attributes and circumstances and create new possibilities for yourself. You can *monetize your ideas* using personal innovation, creativity and entrepreneurship, and in so doing regain some sense of personal financial control.

Though we haven't typically viewed ideas in and of themselves as elements of economic currency, doing so is a way for boomers to create something new out of the personal assets they already possess. There is something appealing about viewing actionable ideas as fuel for creating independence. Each of us already has ideas that can be pressed into service at a moment's notice if we simply raise our level of awareness and allow our creativity to go to work for us.

Economist Paul Romer comments, "We are not used to thinking of ideas as economic goods, but they are surely the most significant ones that we produce . . . Economic growth occurs whenever people take resources and rearrange them in ways that are more valuable . . . [It] springs from better recipes not just from more cooking."[45] I suggest that "better ingredients"—our best ideas, and those that leverage our strengths and uniqueness—are an important part of the foundation for an upward shift in personal success and, in a larger sense, a contribution to economic growth.

Another currency we already possess is the knowledge accumulated from our unique experiences in business and in life. Right now there is likely someone in your community

---

[45] Romer, Paul. 1993. Ideas and things. *The Economist*, September 11.

who needs knowledge that you have at the top of your mind. One potential way to begin monetizing this kind of individual currency is to join a time bank or equivalent organization. A time bank is a place for the barter exchange of your services for other goods or services that you need. In an opinion piece in *The New York Times*, Tina Rosenberg wrote:

> The value of a time bank during a time of high unemployment is obvious. It is a way for underemployed people to put their skills to work to get things they need. (During the Great Depression, a group of men living in a Hooverville of unlaid sewer pipe in California began a barter exchange that eventually had 100,000 members.) Many time banks have a large percentage of members who are older and living on a fixed income. "The difference it makes to have a handyman come out and do a repair for the cost of materials could be the difference between being able to purchase medicine or not," said Barbara Huston, the president and chief executive of Partners in Care, a time bank based near Baltimore. "Getting a ride to the doctor and saving $30 to $50 in transport costs might mean being able to buy all their vegetables.[46]

This is but one instance in which the term *free agency* refers to far more than the status of highly-paid athletes in a position to negotiate even higher pay by leaving their current team and fans behind in favor of a deal that better serves their personal interest. Free agency for mere mortals can be the foundation for a new generation of *elderpreneurs*. It holds the promise of a rebirth of self-reliance in work that

---

[46]Rosenberg, Tina. 2011. Where All Work is Created Equal. *The New York Times*, September 15, Opinion Pages.

can directly address our individual economic requirements.

The good news is that we don't have to be part of traditional employment systems, whatever those may be considered today. We can create our own work styles and participate in economic systems placing a premium on our unique talents and skills. We can be part of the job creation answer for our economy, one free agent boomer at a time.

Chapter 24

Only the Dead Do What They Do

They're not the best at what they do.
They're the only ones that do what they do.
Bill Graham

Bill Graham[47] scrawled this phrase (referring to the Grateful Dead) on a cardboard sign outside a San Francisco concert venue, thereby succinctly conveying the concept of *optimal uniqueness*. In a time when self-reliance and finding our own unique personal advantage is a vital pursuit, this is a particularly provocative thought.

The first time I read this quote I thought, "What a great perspective. I certainly understand that this principle would apply if you're Jerry Garcia and you've fronted the Grateful Dead for thirty years. I mean, who else could possibly be in a position to do what they do?" It makes complete sense that with persistent repetition (estimated at thirty years, 2,318 shows, 408 songs played a total of 37,118 times) you would eventually, inevitably, become the best performer of your music. But, how could what they did possibly apply to the rest of us?

---

[47]Bill Graham was an American impresario and rock concert promoter from the 1960s until his death in 1991.

Repetition is Not (Necessarily) Boring

How about this for a perspective? Jerry Garcia said, "I've always been a musician and into improvising and it's like I consider life to be a continuous series of improvisations."

Not a bad way to view a vagabond lifestyle that might appear from afar to have been nothing but endless monotony—the epitome of life in the form of endless highway miles and indistinguishable concert venues. Many of us have held positions where repetition and routine have been the order of the day. Until now, I hadn't considered that such repetition could be reframed as a continuing opportunity for "improvisation."

Most of us view doing the same thing over and over as boring. It is much more powerful (and palatable) to turn a routine process into ongoing *experimentation* as a way of finding fresh insights and perspectives. If you need a concept to help reframe your perception of your work or something else that seems tedious and boring, try viewing it through the lens of striving for *mastery through repetition*, with the added spice of improvisation to keep it interesting. (See Chapter 26, *Mastery*, for more on this subject.)

Crushed Pineapple

"They're not the best at what they do. They're the only ones that do what they do" described a group of musicians who personified the peace and love (and drug and music)

culture of 1960s Haight-Ashbury in San Francisco. I share
with you this excerpt from a long interview Jerry Garcia gave
to Jann Wenner and Charles A. Reich for *Rolling Stone*
magazine in the early seventies[48]:

> I had an old car when I got out of the Army, and we [Jerry
> and Robert Hunter, Garcia's lyricist] were in East Palo Alto
> sort of coincidentally. There was a coffee house, 'cause of
> Stanford, university town and all that, and we were hang-
> ing out at the coffee house and ran into each other. We had
> our two cars in an empty lot in East Palo Alto where they
> were both broken. Neither of them ran any more but we
> were living in them. Hunter had these big tins of crushed
> pineapple that he'd gotten from the Army, like five or six
> big tins, and I had this glove compartment full of plastic
> spoons and we had this little cooperative scene eating this
> crushed pineapple day after day and sleeping in the cars
> and walking around. He played a little guitar, we started
> singin' and playin' together just for something to do. And
> then we played our first professional gig. We got five bucks
> apiece.

Shortly thereafter, the traveling show that became the
Journey of the Dead was launched. The selection of the name
that would stick with them for thirty years was equally
improbable:

> We never decided to be the Grateful Dead. What happened
> was the Grateful Dead came up as a suggestion because we
> were at Phil's house one day. He had a big Oxford Diction-

[48]Wenner, Jann S. & Reich, Charles. 1972. The Rolling Stone Interview: Jerry Garcia, Part I. Rolling Stone, January 20.

ary I opened it up and the first thing I saw was the "grateful dead." It said that on the page and it was so astonishing. It was truly weird, a truly weird moment. I didn't like it really, I just found it to be really powerful . . . then people started calling us that and it just started, it just got out, Grateful Dead, Grateful Dead.

Jerry Garcia became a legendary figure in music, a humble but larger-than-life personality. The Grateful Dead was hugely successful as an entertainment act, made an impact on millions of people's lives, and was representative of a type of freedom that helped keep the magic of the 1960s and 1970s going for millions of boomer adults.

You might be envious, or thinking "I could never do what he did...?" He *was* a special and unique soul never to be replicated. Just like you. His beginnings were not especially auspicious. He was an active and sometimes repentant drug user and experimenter, which had him in and out of rehab centers during his adult life. What he did more than anything else though, was persist at doing what he loved doing most. He pursued his music every day and continued doing so for over thirty years, until his death from a heart attack at the age of fifty-three.

If you believe your circumstances are overwhelming, that you have nothing to work with, nowhere to go and nothing you can do to create a new life, let's recap the early part of Jerry's story:

- He lived in a car in a vacant lot in Palo Alto (while near but not attending Stanford University.)

- He subsisted on canned pineapple which he ate with a plastic spoon.

- He was a guitar player with a missing finger.

- The name of the band was selected by opening a dictionary to a random page.

- His first paying gig netted him and his buddy $5 apiece.

By most standards, this is not an auspicious foundation for success, but it was certainly a beginning—the first step in what became a very long musical and pop culture journey. Of course if you tried to follow the identical path blazed by Jerry Garcia and the Grateful Dead yourself, I am pretty sure that it would not yield the same results.

Each of our paths is different but alive with the promise of accessing the uniqueness which makes us *the only ones that do what we do*. What could that look like for you? What ideas have you been harboring for years that could be the ignition required to feel good about *really living* your remaining years?

Uniqueness Need Not be Strangeness

What I am suggesting is that a deep look into ourselves and our circumstances—no matter what they may have been or are today—cannot help but reveal something unique. Just as there is not another Jerry Garcia, there is not another you. He made his way out of what many of us would consider to be pretty adverse circumstances. He put one foot in front of the other and continued to take steps in the general direction of his dream.

Garcia expressed a remarkably grounded personal perspective in the *Rolling Stone* interview: "I don't have a personal philosophy . . . all I have is an ability to perceive cycles . . . and I think that things happen in a more or less cyclical way and the thing is being able to maintain your equilibrium while the cycles are in their most disadvantageous places and that seems a function of time."

There were cycles in his life that didn't have anything to do with unemployment and savings rates, foreclosed mortgages, or an uncertain future for Social Security and Medicare. But you have to love the idea of maintaining "...your equilibrium while the cycles are in their most disadvantageous places." If that isn't a powerful, relevant perspective to apply to our times, I don't know what is.

The mastery achieved by Garcia and the Grateful Dead was founded on repetition and improvisation. This *consistency with variation* is what tens of thousands of repeat concertgoers went to see and hear. The band was also aware of the stagnation that could set in without taking time out to regain perspective and re-energize from time to time.

In the *Rolling Stone* interview, Garcia put it this way: "There were one or two years back there when we toured too much and we became mechanical. We began to see that there's a cycle that occurs: you're interested in what you're doing, and then you get disinterested in it. And then it changes and you get interested again. It's a matter of being able to leave space for those changes to happen; and to be in something which will provide you with an open end in which to change."

As you consider the creation that is the rest of your life, there can be everything right about continuing at work in which you have achieved a level of mastery and comfort. Whether you are a teacher, truck driver, investment banker, pilot or retail clerk, when you have mastered your work you need to refresh your perspective from time to time.

You have the ability to improvise as a way of accessing fresh energy and doing so can be the difference between burnout (and potentially walking away from a generally positive situation) and a genuine sense of renewal. Stepping away for just a little while may permit you to continue performing at a high level, providing your singular brand of expertise and value. Call it your own form of *consistency with variation*.

Look for a way to be the only one who does what you do in the way that you do it. It *is* there inside you waiting for your discovery. Anyone willing to take a single step out of their comfort zone and in the direction of a new potential incarnation has this opportunity. I did this myself at age *sixty*, when I finally discovered what—in the entire world—only *I* am able to do in the way that I do it. (I am sure counterpoints could be argued—but this is what I believe and how

I deliver high level service to others.)

Whether you are younger or older than me—it is a choice available to you. I can relate from my experience that with this discovery I went from being naturally curious and *interested* in life, to being *fully committed* to *living it* every moment for the rest of my days.

Chapter 25

The Truth in Game-Changing

In a time of universal deceit,
telling the truth is a revolutionary act.
George Orwell

Most of us aren't yet committed to planning how to spend our finite remaining amount of earthly time. If we have thought about it, we may still be wondering how to begin. In this chapter we look at the paradigm of business planning to shed some light on planning for our personal lives.

My perspective arises out of the high-impact transformational work I do for companies and high-powered individuals. It is based upon a keen eye and well-developed intuition, which are the result of extensive experience, encompassing both successes and failures.

I have developed the ability and willingness to speak the unadulterated truth about what I see, and to clearly explain what I believe must be done to immediately shift the *status quo*. It is not much of a stretch to approach the ongoing development, management and planning of our personal lives (the business of living) in much the same way as we might for a commercial enterprise.

The Truth Will Set You Free

Sometimes those who most need to hear the truth receive only lies and distorted versions of it from those upon whom they rely. There are many reasons for this on the part of the potential "truth-teller," including a desire to ingratiate rather than truly help, the need to preserve a job or friendship, fear of appearing hostile and so on. These often short-term, self-interested reasons can trump the long-term greater good, particularly if the person who needs to hear the truth is also the type who will then act on it.

It is also true that some of the people who could most benefit from hearing the unvarnished truth are so reactionary that revealing it to them is the equivalent of walking in bare feet across hot coals. They keep so much distance between themselves and others, wearing protective layers of armor and resisting advice so vigorously that, understandably, there are not a lot of volunteers for the job.

Sometimes it is difficult to see the truth about what is not working in a game we have been playing for a long time. Over time we tend to lose objectivity, forgetting that disruption of our routines can sometimes serve our best interests. We become weighted down by what we already know. We make decisions based on routine and reaction rather than reflection. Both businesses and individuals can usually benefit from inviting an outsider to provide objectivity, a fresh perspective and the opportunity to help shake up the *status quo*.

For a company, such perspective can be provided by a seasoned consultant (for the management team, the board or selected executives) or by a new employee sufficiently brave or naïve to be willing to act as a change agent. For an individual, a handpicked, experienced coach or mentor can deliver service matched with your readiness, needs and personality. People in these roles can serve as powerful catalysts for helping cut through malaise and dysfunction, exposing the lies that keep people and organizations stuck in neutral or worse.

As individuals, it is *possible* to do this for ourselves with the right amount of objectivity, commitment and effort. But sometimes getting to the starting line as our own change agent is a bit like restarting an exercise routine: you have to get to the gym before you can start the workout. Some people are disciplined enough to get there without a push, and some are not.

From my work with companies, I know that some of the important answers that have eluded those in the business are already present, and in some cases downright obvious to someone not a part of the existing team. Change often requires an outsider's perspective and a willingness to boldly challenge the *status quo*. It often takes a different viewpoint to break through the blockages and show the way forward. But the real work must ultimately be done by the businesses or individuals committed to turning a new vision into reality, through their daily commitment and effort. This means that they also have to be motivated as change agents in their own service.

I have worked with some high-powered executives who on a personal level were in the same "stuck" position as their company. In those cases, what they needed first and foremost was someone to tell them the truth about *themselves*. They were used to people saying, "Yes!" and telling them what they wanted to hear.

As mentioned above, these individuals had in many ways encouraged this behavior by ignoring or humiliating those who offered them the opportunity to hear the truth. An executive—or in fact, anyone—in this kind of position needs someone to highlight their false beliefs, to correct their misperceptions of their failures, and to show them the personal power that is at their disposal if they would just get out of their own way.

Immediacy of Action

My belief about most transformational change is that while it must be thoughtful, it need not always be lengthy or overly sequential. It can be brought into being in a single, fluid motion encompassing an assessment of historical and current reality, prioritizing what needs to be done, and taking first steps into action. In many situations it is possible for these tasks to be done somewhat concurrently. When the feedback from the first moves is available for review, course adjustments can be made immediately, while the creation and reinvention process continues with all due speed. This is as true for individuals as it is for companies.

In a business situation, I insist that my entry as an agent for changing the *status quo* be accompanied by an authoritative commitment from the highest level of organizational leadership. This comes with an understanding that full support for a process of change—which usually requires disruption and some "breakage" of the existing structure—must be unequivocal and consistent. Without it, the whole activity can be a waste of time.

On an individual level, the same kind of unequivocal commitment is necessary in order to get outside the comfort zone of your *status quo*. This is sometimes difficult, even when you are aware that your current state of being is working against you. If you invite a game-changer or transformational leader into your life, the good ones will insist upon a mutual commitment to your doing the work that is required for success. Anyone worth their salt doesn't just want to be paid—they want their efforts to *make a difference*.

The entry of a committed change agent into a situation requiring decisive triage is often uncomfortable for those serving the *status quo*. As such, it is not surprising that the arrival of such an agent of change often engenders fierce resistance. Because I know this is going to be the case when I walk into a situation, the responsible board members and executives have to recognize the need for *real change* (not a consulting report with recommendations for *possible* consideration by the company at some unspecified point in the future). They must have already made a high-level commitment to immediately do what is required to move in a new direction.

* * *

Intolerance of the status quo and an unequivocal commitment to change are necessary for the accomplishment of significant personal transformation.

* * *

Why? In order to effect rapid change, existing rules, hierarchies, respect for keepers of tribal knowledge and even superficial civility may have to go out the window to allow sunlight and fresh air back in again. Existing energy being spent on resistance to change has to be redirected into the change process. This shift cannot be equivocal.

If you commit (and recommit daily) you can change your game almost immediately. The question is, how much do you care about changing things, and for how long can and will you maintain that level of caring? Do you care enough to awaken each morning and commit to advancing your highest priorities in work and life in some way? Or will you be comfortable reacting to whatever happens to you during the day, remaining entrenched in your comfort zone?

Chapter 26

Mastery

Only one who devotes himself to a cause with
his whole strength and soul can be a true master.
For this reason mastery demands all of a person.
Albert Einstein

I love the concept of *mastery*. I even love the sound of the word. *Mastery*! It implies an expertise that has been carefully forged and then aged to perfection. It conveys an aura of trust and safety.

A person who has achieved a level of mastery at anything has attained a high degree of proficiency borne of a deep, long-term understanding of their chosen specialty, its challenges, nuances and opportunities for innovation. In many areas we might say that, "If something difficult is made to appear easy, it is due to the mastery of the doer." Mastery suggests a depth of knowledge, experience and capability that places one at the elite level of their game.

You already have uniqueness; as a human, you were born with it. You have gifts unlike those possessed by any others. Perhaps they have yet to reveal themselves to you because the need has not arisen or because you have not been motivated to identify them. But now is the perfect moment to explore your uniqueness and to then use what you discover to productively engage with life in the years ahead. You may even choose to take *your game* to the level of mastery.

Overnight Success Usually Isn't

In his book, *Outliers*, Malcolm Gladwell cites a study by Anders Ericsson and comments, "The curious thing about Ericsson's study is that he and his colleagues couldn't find any "naturals" — musicians who could float effortlessly to the top while practicing a fraction of the time that their peers did. Nor could they find "grinds," people who worked harder than everyone else and yet just didn't have what it takes to break into the top ranks.

Their research suggested that once you have enough ability to get into a top music school, the thing that distinguishes one performer from another is how hard he or she works. That's it. What's more, the people at the very top don't just work much harder than everyone else. They work much, much harder."[49]

If you are already experienced in something (or several somethings) related to your objective for mastery, additional effort could get you to the top even faster. If you decide today (or next week or even next year) that you want to master something to make the rest of your days more

---

[49]Gladwell, Malcolm. 2008. *Outliers*. New York: Little, Brown and Company.

meaningful, productive, interesting, profitable—or all of the above—it is well within your capacity to do so. In most cases, making a bold move in the direction of mastery now will leave you with many years during which to pursue and enjoy your chosen course and its rewards.

* * *

The mere effort in striving for the level of mastery— whether or not you ultimately reach it—will open doors to possibilities that would otherwise remain closed.

* * *

As George Leonard wrote in *Mastery: The Keys to Success and Long-Term Fulfillment*, "Ultimately, practice *is* the path of mastery." He also wrote, "Almost without exception, those we know as masters are dedicated to the fundamentals of their calling. They are zealots of practice, connoisseurs of the small, incremental step. At the same time—and here's the paradox—these people are precisely the ones who are likely to challenge previous limits, to take risks for the sake of higher performance, and seem to become obsessive at times in that pursuit."[50]

It is unsurprising that the important things we accomplish in life are almost always the result of pushing the limits of our existing envelope of personal performance. Our most compelling and rewarding outputs are the result of

---

[50]Leonard, George. 1992. *Mastery: The Keys to Success and Long-Term Fulfillment*. New York: Penguin Books USA.

getting up and out of our comfort zone. (Take another look at Chapter 2, *"Listen to Me, Dammit!"*)

How Long Do Whales Live?

The same commitment to continuous practice and persistence holds for learning. Between 1750 and 1900, total human knowledge merely doubled. Today, the growth of knowledge is estimated to be occurring some 100 times faster. The entire sum of all known human knowledge is now expected to double every year and a half. By 2020 it is estimated that knowledge could be doubling approximately every month and a half.

Failing to learn something new each and every day puts you further and further behind in the human race. This is especially true as an American boomer, where the competition for available resources and income is dramatically escalating among your peers. The competition from the generations behind the boomers will become fiercer as well. Embracing technological advances is crucial for accessing the information you need to stay relevant in the mainstream and in your service to others. (Remember the concepts explored in Chapter 22, *Technology: You Can't Win If You Don't Play.*)

Merely acting on your curiosity provides life-extending mental stimulation and exercise. The answers you need or want to questions relating to most areas of human endeavor are available in a few clicks on your choice of digital appliance, be it a smartphone, computer or tablet (all of which are getting faster, cheaper and easier to use).

You can quickly access answers to questions such as the one posed above, which occurred to me while watching a Pacific Life television commercial featuring magnificent video footage of whales in action. I asked myself, "I wonder how long whales live?" I found the answer in about thirty seconds on my Apple iPhone: Whales live about fifty years on average, but humpbacks live as long as 125 years.

Perhaps we don't need to know the answers to such questions to remain relevant or to better serve others, but when we pursue our curiosity we keep our minds open and well-fed, ready for new and possibly even lifelong endeavors. (Obviously, traditional, tangible materials such as books made of paper are also ways of accessing knowledge. These increasingly more cumbersome materials—who would ever have thought we would say *books* are becoming cumbersome?—are, however, unlikely to be rapidly updated, are not as readily accessible to people everywhere no matter what they are doing, and take much more time to explore.)

The point is that there are *no credible excuses* for not being able to learn rapidly and continuously. If you don't embrace a daily regimen of knowledge expansion, you are choosing by default to move in the direction of irrelevancy—which in my view is far worse than simply being considered "old."

Fast Learning

Should you as a boomer (or American of any age) decide to pursue a college degree, perhaps finish a Master's, become a lawyer, software programmer, cameraman, actor or coach—you can. Education is available in a wider variety of easily accessible forms than ever before. Education is so ubiquitous that for certain pursuits all you need is a computer (or maybe just a smartphone) and an internet connection. If you are working full time but are committed to advancing your education, you could devote twenty hours a week toward education and still have about forty-five waking hours per week available for other activities.

I had never written a book, but I decided to share my thinking about the themes you are reading about here. I have a full-time consulting and executive coaching practice focused on situations where business and personal transformation must typically be achieved with a high degree of urgency. My work requires me to assimilate knowledge extremely quickly in order to move into action and be of maximum value as soon as possible. (It helps, of course, that this ability is part of my uniqueness, something I continue to cultivate and strive for in the direction of mastery.)

I also travel almost every week and have a family that includes a teenager at home. I still managed to find enough hours—early mornings and evenings, later at night (actually, at all times of the night) and on weekends—to complete this book in about six months. In my case, I considered the subject matter timely and important, so it wasn't difficult staying motivated. I also relished applying my gift for learning at a rapid rate to the new challenge of becoming an author. "Finding time" can be done for the things we really value.

"Man, I'm Good."

You can observe people all around you who are accomplished at what they do, be it domestic or office work, retailing, construction, transportation, full-time parenting, volunteering and so on. Those who provide efficient and exceptional service are consistently in greater demand, get paid more and are happier doing what they do. A commitment to service coupled with just a bit of extra effort will also yield *positive self-esteem*.

Self-esteem is being sufficiently well-equipped to cope with the basic demands of life—and feeling good about it. When you cope better you enhance your ability to overcome obstacles and to reach higher levels of accomplishment. Low self-esteem results from being and staying stuck, from being unable or unwilling (or too numb) to identify and overcome the hurdles that are a part of every human condition. If you think back to Chapter 13, *Choosing Ownership*, you can quickly identify owners and victims based upon the level of self-esteem they exhibit. Owners possess positive self-esteem that helps them compete well for limited available resources.

In a 1994 essay (which could have been written just yesterday) Nathaniel Branden wrote, "We now live in a global economy characterized by rapid change, accelerating scientific and technological breakthroughs, and an unprecedented level of competitiveness. These developments create demands for higher levels of education and training. These developments also create new demands on our psychological resources. Specifically, *these developments ask for a greater capacity for innovation, self-management, personal responsibility, and self-direction."*[51] (Emphasis added.)

Those with positive self-esteem are more inclined to overcome their limiting beliefs to push beyond their comfort zones. They are willing to embrace higher degrees of discomfort in order to move to higher levels of personal performance. This creates the opportunity for them to achieve greater levels of satisfaction in all aspects of life.

We have available for the taking the opportunity of combining the business of making a living with our gifts of uniqueness. This can lead to the years ahead being marked by creative exploration on many levels, rather than by mere labor and constant worry about the negative what-ifs. Branden wrote, *"Positive self-esteem operates, in effect, as providing resistance, strength, and a capacity for regeneration.* When self-esteem is low, our resilience in the face of life's problems is diminished. We tend to be more influenced by the desire to avoid pain than to experience joy; negatives have more power over us than positives."* (Emphasis added.)

If you believe that because you are fifty-five or seventy

---

[51]Branden, Nathaniel. Our Urgent Need for Self-Esteem. <http://www.nathanielbranden.com/2011/06/our-urgent-need-for-self-esteem/>

it is *too late* to start something, please understand that you are simply saying "I don't want to" rather than "I can't." This is your *individual choice* based on a perception that the time and resources you have left are of little value. You are in fact making a decision by default to "just wait it out." Wait what out? What in the world could possibly be good about waiting in a state of inertia for the exhalation of your last breath?

We have all witnessed people of every age literally and figuratively stuck in this waiting mode. They drum their fingers, aimlessly shaking one leg crossed atop the other, or maybe their eyes are closed, head propped back, mouth open. They sleep their way through airplane travel, movies, meetings, even parties. They may love the television remote more than the people in their lives (and hold it more closely).

Of course, we have all waited to one extent or another during periods in our lifetimes. Don't be overly critical if you've recently caught yourself at this. But if you are waiting at this moment, please stop it, and stop it now. Waiting to engage is a waste of your perfectly good life—no matter how young or old you may be.

Age as a biological state has very little to do with our actual ability to *play* the game of life. What is relevant is getting your brain in gear and overcoming your resistance to taking just *one single step*. Without question, that step will move you to a different perspective, thereby providing a different access point to your future.

Curiosity, learning and mastery are inextricably intertwined with positive self-esteem. Strive for the former and you will be rewarded with the latter. Seek relevance, expand your personal knowledge, engage with life and strive for mastery in your chosen field.

We are here. Time is passing. The end of life is closer now than it was just a moment ago. If you choose to increase the intensity of your game now, you will move yourself in the direction of mastery—and feel better about yourself too.

Chapter 27

It's Not Too Late

*Nowadays most people die of a sort of
creeping common sense, and discover when it is too late
that the only things one never regrets are one's mistakes.*
Oscar Wilde

Most of our significant growth is achieved by engaging with challenges, crises, obstacles and failures. Often it arises from our bold reaction to being told "No" or "You can't." In many periods in history, the elements of emergency, danger and crisis providing grist for such growth were more obviously threatening than they are today. In fact, until recently most Americans have felt pretty comfortable for most of their lives.

But at the moment there are highly visible reasons for almost all of us to feel uncomfortable—at the very least. Recall the survey results in Chapter 9 (*Protect Yourself at All Times!*) indicating that approximately fifty percent of Americans definitely or likely couldn't come up with $2,000 within thirty days. Add to this precarious financial condition the fact that seventy-five million boomers are inexorably marching toward and through age sixty-five. *All* of us will eventually have spending requirements different from those we had when we were younger and these will come at a time when many of us will be living on more fixed incomes.

As a consequence, in the near future even greater stress will be placed on healthcare and other support systems that already aren't up to the job. Many in our nation are now or will be affected by the absence of credible, predictable, trusted government financial subsidies, programs and support. The effects of these gaps on boomers will certainly cascade down to the younger generations.

By any measure, our society is in a state of disruption that will continue for several decades. If these problems remain unaddressed proactively at a personal level, the result will be increasing fear, worry and inertia for a good part of the population.

But opportunity is always present during periods of major disruption. This is certainly true today, when we have the possibility—both as individuals and as members of society at large—of participating in the reorientation, renewal and restructuring of our world. The future is bright for those of us willing to think for ourselves, live up to our commitments and take control of our actions. It is there for those who are ready to be creative and bold.

I changed my own game and life-tested the transformational principles and processes discussed in this book while going through a pivotal period of transition in my life. This shift was made by me at *sixty*, an age when a lot of people have traditionally been looking for an exit ramp from the freeway of life. My story is proof that it can be done.

I came to the realizations I have shared with you here about the changes in the American economic landscape and future, and the impact of those changes on me as an individual. This understanding moved me to determine the points of intersection between what I most enjoyed doing and where I believed I could provide the most value for others. I pushed myself to explore and understand my uniqueness and tap into creativity that was waiting to get to work.

Instead of the formal employment to which I had defaulted for much of my life, I chose the life of a *free agent.* I started my own, focused consulting practice. (See Chapter 23, *Free Agency.*) I chose to offer a one-of-a-kind service to others in situations that seemed to them to be beyond perplexing—even unsolvable—but which for me represented opportunities to be of significant assistance. I also made a personal commitment to work only with people committed to making the move from *wherever they were at the moment—good, bad, neutral—to great,* but who didn't know what steps to take.

I personally chose to utilize constant awareness of my mortality to drive better, faster and more thoughtful decisions about every aspect of my life. (A focus on mortality may not work for you, but there are plenty of other options available for driving yourself into action.) My self-talk now sounds something like this, "I am the owner of my life." "I choose to do this." "I choose not to do that." This approach brings clarity to the fact that I am exercising choice and decision-making power. These decisions, as much as possible, are based upon telling myself the truth about where I am and where I am going.

Other ways of getting into motion (and out of being stuck) include thoughtful commitments, serving others as a primary focus, moving toward mastery (of anything), and discovering and leveraging your differences—your uniqueness.

Many of the points made in *Life Expectancy* represent tools to help you eradicate fear, to get you out of the way of your own success. Some of these concepts, articulated in previous chapters, include choosing ownership over victimhood, being truthful with yourself, preferring action over hope, embracing independence and self-reliance as ways of being, finding and taking first steps, and living in the *now*.

Throughout this book I have encouraged you to *move*, to *get into motion*, because I believe that doing so is a virtual panacea—the antidote to almost everything that is in our way. Commitments, mastery, playing to win, shifting your mind—all are accessible and actionable if you can overcome inertia—even just a little to begin.

There is no silver bullet here. We are not all created equal in terms of intelligence, ambition or resources. We don't (and can't) have an equivalent level of education, support or experience. But what we all have available to us are creativity, energy and the ability to commit. If you choose to embrace the principles set forth here, you will have reached a legitimate starting line for intentionally and proactively changing your game for the rest of your life

Whether you choose to actively engage in a creative process for living or not, the ultimate and irrevocable end of your game of life is waiting for you. Until that moment, you have the opportunity to choose whether the balance of your days will be boring or fearful, interesting or energizing, or whatever else you want it to be. The richness of your life from this moment forward can be determined by the results of purposeful decision-making you can address immediately.

The good news is that the arrival of permanent disruption and challenge in our world means that there will be new winners—a *lot* of them. If you are ready to change your game, to take it to a higher level—maybe even to the top— you can choose it. You already have everything you need.

Great lives come from owning our thinking, our choices and our actions. These elements are the foundation for self-reliant living and personal mastery of our circumstances, environments and outcomes.

There is risk in life whether we want it or not. Security in today's world is defined by our readiness to be creative and bold in the face of whatever may come. It's never too late to begin creating the kinds of differences that can make your life more meaningful—to you and to others.

About the Author

William (Will) Keiper has served as Chairman of the Board, Chief Executive Officer, President and as a trusted advisor for a variety of public and private companies. Through his consulting firm FirstGlobal® Partners, Mr. Keiper serves committed individuals, company owners, executives, investors and others in urgently resolving their most challenging issues. In situations where the *status quo* will no longer be tolerated, he will accelerate the change process through rapid assessment and the speed and urgency of implementation.

He earned a business degree with honors from Eastern Illinois University, a law degree from the Sandra Day O'Connor College of Law at Arizona State University, and a Master's degree from the Thunderbird School of Global Management.

The author can be engaged to present the "live version" of *Life Expectancy*. For details and scheduling, please contact LE@firstglobalpartners.com.

<u>A Parting Gift</u>

As a final thought for your consideration, I offer you the complete text of the poem "Risks" by William Arthur Ward, first referenced in Chapter 2, *"Listen to Me Dammit!"*:

Risks

To laugh is to risk appearing the fool.
To weep is to risk appearing sentimental.
To reach out to another is to risk involvement.
To expose feelings is to risk exposing your true self.
To place your dreams, ideas before a crowd is to risk their
    loss.
To love is to risk not being loved in return.
To live is to risk dying.
To hope is to risk despair.
To try is to risk failure.
But risks must be taken, because the greatest hazard in life is to
    risk nothing.
The person who risks nothing, does nothing, has nothing, and is
    nothing.
They may avoid suffering and sorrow, but they cannot learn,
    feel, change, grow, love, live.
Chained by their certitudes, they are a slave: they have forfeited
    their freedom.
Only a person who risks is truly free.

* * *

CPSIA information can be obtained at www.ICGtesting.com
Printed in the USA
BVOW030926050312

284345BV00002B/2/P